Working on the Fault Line

Greta Bradley and Jill Manthorpe

VENTURE PRESS

BASW website: http://www.basw.co.uk

Published by
VENTURE PRESS
16 Kent Street
Birmingham
B5 6RD

British Library Cataloguing-in-Publication Data
A catalogue record for this book is available from the British Library

ISBN   1 86178 043 5   (paperback)

Cover design by:
Western Arts
194 Goswell Road
London
EC1V 7DT

Printed in Great Britain

Contents   Page

Introduction
Greta Bradley and Jill Manthorpe

A popular image characterising the problems of contemporary health and welfare services has been remarkably resilient over time. The situation of an older person, usually a woman, occupying a hospital bed is seen as wasteful and unnecessary. Such people are often referred to as 'bed-blockers' and appear blamed for their own predicament. This book builds on this powerful image to explore the world of health-related social work. This activity is assuming new importance at the very time when medical and technological developments seem to offer a vision of advanced medical progress. The reality of health services at the beginning of the twenty-first century is that they must encompass both the demands of an ageing population and a public with high expectations of medical treatment throughout the life course. The majority of National Health Service (NHS) expenditure (80 per cent) is on the care of either the very young (children aged under six) and those in the last three years of life (Office for National Statistics, 1999). One mechanism for responding to enhanced demand has been to control entry and exit to hospital care. This book explores the implications for social work activity of these major restructurings. Our emphasis is on adult services, in particular those for older people who are important consumers of health and social care services. We offer a selection of perspectives on practice issues for social workers and those who seek a greater understanding of their world.

Policy documents in recent years have not specifically addressed the needs of older people, although as we write the Government's initiative for 'Better Government for Older People' is under way and the Royal Commission on Long-term Care for the Elderly (Sutherland, 1999) has submitted its report. The NHS and Community Care Act 1990 was, in essence, a response to government anxiety about older people and the dangers perceived to arise from their consumption of welfare. Recent evidence from the National Beds Inquiry notes that two-thirds of hospital beds are occupied by people aged 65 or over (DoH, 2000a). These dangers, portraying older people as potential means of bankrupting the welfare state, echo the victimising approach of seeing them as 'bed-blockers' within local settings such as hospital wards. Ironically, we are now receiving persuasive evidence that older people are in fact discriminated against in health services (Gilchrist, 1999) and that the quality of care they receive in some hospital wards is poor (Help the Aged, 1999).

This book is written for practitioners, managers, students and trainers. It is designed to be an accessible text presenting a series of research studies to illuminate practice and to inform policy development. Many research studies

1

find difficulty in reaching and influencing practice. However, it is our belief that practitioners are keen to learn from research, particularly because there is such wide variation between localities. Learning from other areas is an important element in enabling practitioners to develop some objectivity about their practice. Self-reflection is much encouraged within social work, and reflecting on the work of others provides a context for such activity. It needs, too, to be informed by user and carer perspectives as other books in this series will confirm.

The changing role of health-related social work

Change of task and development of role has been an integral part of health-related social work throughout the last century. At a simple level these developments can be chronicled by the change of title. For example, in 1895 Mary Stewart was first appointed to the Royal Free Hospital in London to work as an almoner. This post was a direct consequence of a House of Lords Select Committee Report in 1892 on the 'abuse' of hospitals in the metropolis (Baraclough, 1995). The influential Charity Organization Society had argued that its casework model of preventing pauperisation should be extended to almoners who would 'gatekeep' access to free hospital care (Parry and Parry, 1979). It seconded Stewart as an almoner, to distinguish the 'deserving' from the 'undeserving' (p.28). As Hall (1965) observed, she occupied a 'dingy, dark, unventilated corridor of the out-patient department' (p.136), but Stewart herself wished to create a service to help patients and their families with special needs and problems arising from their illnesses. Other hospitals followed this approach. Although exclusively a female occupation until comparatively recently, almoners quickly became viewed as an 'elite' occupation, since its personnel were salaried, trained and had social status. Walton (1975) characterised almoners as 'middle-and upper-class women, insisting on high intellectual and moral standards, the greater number of them still single' (p.156). Following a casework approach, they extended their activities to promote access to treatment and broader public health issues, particularly among maternal and child welfare cases.

The work quickly became professionalised, with almoners forming a Hospital Almoners Committee in 1903, setting up training and recruitment processes through the Hospital Almoners Council in 1907 and working with the London School of Economics to award certificates of training in 1912. During the First World War, the role of almoners was encouraged in relation to its casualties while in the aftermath of the depression almoners were again used to work with deserving economic casualties. The Hospital Almoners Association was formed in 1922 with 51 members and in 1929 almoners were appointed to some municipal hospitals and tuberculosis (TB) sanitoria under local government legislative reform. With the founding of the NHS in 1948, almoners were freed from financial assessment to 'engage fully on the important medical social work for which she had been specially trained' (Ministry of Health, 1948, cited in Hall 1965). Their concentration on work with people suffering from TB and their families was sustained, however, as the Younghusband report into social work, recruitment and training (1959) confirmed. Almost half of the almoners surveyed were engaged on after-care work in TB services. Interestingly, again, most were single women. Younghusband provided an important ideal type definition of the almoner (para. 433):

> The professionally trained almoner is a caseworker in a medical setting . . .
> She assesses the personal, family or social factors relevant to medical diagnosis and treatment, and helps patients to deal with these stresses, and to try to solve problems which may be causing anxiety and strain, or which delay response to medical treatment. She is trained to help people in the acceptance of, or adjustment to, illness or disability and to modify disturbed, emotional or family relationships . . . Generally, and not only in relation to tuberculosis, her work falls into four-related stages – supplying information about the resources available, arranging services or material assistance, giving support through the crisis of diagnosis and illness, and providing casework help. (para.433)

Almoners were to remain few and far between, however, moving to be jointly employed by the health and local authorities and increasingly termed medical social workers. In one of the rare detailed studies of social work at the time, Jefferys (1965) surveyed all social work staff in the county of Buckinghamshire, including almoners. She found 22 staff employed in hospitals as almoners, their assistants or psychiatric social workers, which she regarded as understaffed. As a consequence, she considered their work fell short of intensive casework as 'the hospital was an unsatisfactory base for establishing close relationships between social workers and client' (p.114). It is clear that even without the previous pressures of financial assessment, there have always been problems for hospital based social workers in establishing a valid role.

Following the Seebohm Report (1968) and the resulting changes in local government, they were renamed hospital social workers and became employed in 1974 by the local authority. Seebohm had pointed out that 90 per cent of medical social workers were based in hospitals (para. 688) and urged a review of a resource which appeared to the Committee to be expensive and not wholly effective in community based care. Hospital social work, however, was not extensively reviewed. The nature of the work was to be influenced more directly by changing demand. Foremost was the decline in tuberculosis work and the impact of work associated with disabilities and the ageing population. As the National Beds Inquiry (DoH 2000a) discovered, admission rates to hospital among older people are now substantially higher than those of other adults. The fall in length of hospital stay also appears to have levelled out. Other different health-related problems are now evident. People with cancer, people with HIV/Aids, people with addiction-related problems, people with serious head injuries resulting from major traumas have all risen in number. Work in this area requires skills similar to those identified by Younghusband, 40 years earlier, although the social model of disability has challenged the notions of acceptance and personal adjustment. Equally, responses to the diversity of the population in terms of ethnicity, sexuality and acceptance of personal autonomy require sophisticated analyses of equal opportunities and empowerment.

Hospital social workers are well placed to offer a level of expertise which draws on a range of helping and counselling skills. Work with older people and others with long-term health care and nursing needs who no longer remain for extended periods in hospital has assumed a new importance. Their rehabilitation arrangements and discharge planning have become a major responsibility for such social workers and their successors, the care managers; not only for those attached to the so-called geriatric wards but also for those working on medical and surgical wards. With lead responsibility for adult protection proposed for social services departments (DoH, 2000b) in the policy guidance *No Secrets*, new imperatives look set to add further dimensions to the assessment role of health-related social work.

Whether a tension exists between the professional desire to offer a counselling or casework service and the prescribed role of care management will be explored in later sections. It is possible, though, that care management, with its emphasis on meeting eligibility criteria, on the focused assessment of need and financial assessment, constrains health-related social workers from providing a therapeutic or helping service. The five research studies presented here provide evidence of the precarious nature of such work. Equally, while local authority social workers continue to operate within health care settings there may be strains in relationships at professional and agency levels. Pressure, for example, to increase hospital in patient turnover by reliance on social care or family support may be interpreted as detrimental to social well-being. Similarly, care packages put together in a 'safe' and largely untested environment such as a hospital may be viewed with suspicion by colleagues in the field. A Social Services Inspectorate report (DoH, SSI, 1993) classified hospital social work as being located at the interface; this can be interpreted at a variety of levels – interpersonally, interprofessionally and interagency. As Chapter 5 observes, the role of social workers is strongly influenced by these wider changes in welfare provision and in particular to interprofessional and interagency boundaries.

The remotest of periods – the recent past* (* Bennett 1994, p.319).

Recent government statements have directed the NHS and social services to concentrate on sustaining and developing partnerships and effective working together:

> *The Government aims to build a modern, dependable health service with patients having fast access to high quality services based on need . . . Instead of the fragmentation and bureaucracy of the internal market, we are building a system of integrated care, based on partnership. Social services have a key role in that partnership. All too often when people have complex needs spanning both health and social care good quality services are sacrificed for sterile arguments about boundaries.*
> (Foreword, DoH *Partnerships in Action*,1998)

This imperative is not new. Indeed, the history of hospital social work chronicles debates about boundaries and whether the 'right people are in the right place', not only in terms of patients but also in terms of social workers. With the benefit of hindsight it is relatively easy to highlight key moments when opportunities were not taken and mistakes were made. Hinchcliffe (1997) drew attention to some of the missed opportunities and even retrograde steps which have helped undermine effective interdisciplinary – across boundary – working. He lamented that 'until Aneurin Bevan had his difficulties with the doctors, there had been a cross-party government commitment to a coordinated system of voluntary and municipal hospitals based on local government' (p.14). Both he and Lewis and Glennerster (1996) recognised that an opportunity was missed in the 1974 reorganisation of local government when public health departments merged with social services departments. Personnel such as district nurses and health visitors, who remain key players in terms of service provision to vulnerable adults and children, did not move with their old departments but were transferred into health funded settings (Lewis and Glennerster, 1996). Twenty years later, many social services departments have been subsumed into corporate directorates within local authorities. One major change in interagency working is that relationships are now far more important at the level of the individual local authority and health authority. Much attention is now being given to commissioning of joint services and developing understandings of responsibilities at this level. However, the continual lack of coterminosity between local and health authorities helps neither develop effective systems. The 1982 NHS reorganisation removed area health authorities and the opportunities to pull local boundaries together. Local government reorganisation 1995–9 has further fragmented the patchwork of local authorities (Craig and Manthorpe, 1999).

A glimpse at the history of health and social services attempting to work together may reveal a strange series of manoeuvres. Creating coterminous boundaries and working at the interface in common locations are continual challenges. Section 10 of the NHS Reorganisation Act 1973 placed a statutory obligation on health and social services to cooperate in carrying out their respective functions. In 1974 Joint Consultative Committees (JCCs) were introduced to advise the two institutions. Nonetheless, throughout the 1970s and much of the 1980s, initiatives to work together appeared to be undermined by structural factors. Different planning cycles and funding arrangements, different types of accountability between health and social services have made planning and delivery of services hazardous. For example, the annual planning cycles of local government had a poor fit with the five-yearly cycles of the health authorities.

Contrasts in professional cultures and forms of accountability were recognised by the Audit Commission report Making a *Reality of Community Care* (1986). As a response, joint assessments, 'seamless care' and effective partnerships in the development of community care plans were highlighted in the 1990 NHS and Community Care Act (Lewis and Glennerster, 1996). Community Care Plans became the focus for joint planning between agencies. At the level of practice, guidance stressed that it was not the role of government to draw demarcation lines between health and social services, but rather 'the interface between the two is for local discussion and agreement' (DoH, SSI, SWSG, 1991, p.85). However, clearer lines of responsibility were drawn at the level of procedure for hospital discharge of patients entering publicly funded nursing or residential homes, reflecting the transfer of funding responsibility to local authorities in April 1993. 'If a placement is made without the approval of the local authority, the funding responsibility will rest either with the user/patient or the referring agency' (DoH, SSI, SWSG, 1991, p.92).

In the late 1990s the call from government for professionals to heed the 'joined up' agenda would suggest that considerable work remains. Different geographical boundaries remain between health authorities/trusts and the local authorities; in most areas the health authority and or trusts have to relate to more than one social services department. Highly relevant to the health-related

6

social worker is the issue of charging for services. As we have seen, the origins of the profession lie in its means-testing and rationing of resources. *Partnership in Action* (DoH, 1998, section 4.13) confirmed the Government's commitment to keeping health services free at the point of delivery. In contrast, social care is predominantly provided on the basis of a means test. Such charges have had major impact on older people. Older service users continue to express concern that they are required to pay for services delivered by local authorities which are remarkably similar to those provided free through the National Health Service.

Plan of the book

This book provides five research studies focusing on health-related social work and its engagement with hospital, primary and community care. The first study reports on a project which placed social workers within primary health care settings. The move from fundholding general practitioners (GPs) operating within a strict purchaser/provider NHS to primary care groups looks set to confirm the rise in importance of GPs. While much health-related social work in the past has been focused on hospitals, primary care at local level is assuming far greater significance. We know that GPs play a major part in delivering health care for older people living in the community. The potential for partnership at this level may well be judged by the success of this type of initiative.

The second contribution by Sarah Webb and Enid Levin explores day-to-day activities of social work practitioners working in both hospital and locality based settings. Their perspectives form the central focus of this research and the findings offer a unique view of how both sets of social workers spend their time. Of particular interest is their observation that the work of both hospital and community based social workers may be becoming more similar and converging.

Chapter 3 moves to consider hospital social work in the context of care management. Here Jill Manthorpe and Greta Bradley are able to look at examples of work with older people at individual level. Again we provide opportunities to contrast the working practices of those based in health settings with perspectives from those based in the community.

In the next chapter, Bridget Penhale explores one key aspect of hospitals: the accident and emergency department. Many older people and others attend this department which also operates systems to screen or restrict entry to inpatient status. Similarly, staff within accident and emergency departments may refer individuals to social services staff based within the hospital or make other arrangements for social services to be contacted. Hospital discharge problems are also encountered within this setting.

The final research study by Vanessa Malin adopts a policy study approach to continuing care. Long-term care remains a thorny issue for government in terms of expenditure and the complex responsibilities held by the health service, local authorities, families and individuals. This policy case study highlights the continual adjustments to terminology, definition and responsibility.

The title of this book, *Working on the Fault Line* reflects the scale and importance of the debate over the proper relationships between agencies and individual practitioners involved in health and community care. Practitioners often witness the jarring together of such agencies and may find it difficult to appreciate that many levels are involved, particularly when they see and feel some responsibility for difficulties experienced by vulnerable service users. The research studies in this book provide a context to practice and opportunities to reflect on the present, the past and the future.

References

Audit Commission (1986) *Making a Reality of Community Care* London, HMSO

Baraclough, J (1995) 'A cause for celebration' Special Supplement: A hundred years of health related social work, *Professional Social Work*, January, pp 9–12

Bennett, A (1994) *Writing Home* London, Faber and Faber

Craig, G and Manthorpe, J (1999) *Unfinished Business* Bristol, Policy Press

DoH (Department of Health) (1998) *Partnership in Action: new opportunities for joint working between health and social services – a discussion document* London, Department of Health

DoH (2000a) *Shaping the Future NHS: Long term planning for hospitals and related services* London, Department of Health

DoH (2000b) *No Secrets* London, Department of Health

DoH, SSI (Department of Health, Social Services Inspectorate) (1993) *Social Services for Hospital Patients* London, HMSO

DoH, SSI, SO (Department of Health, Social Services Inspectorate, Scottish Office, Social Work Services Group) (1991) *Care Management and Assessment: practitioners' guide* London, HMSO

Gilchrist, C (1999) *Turning Your Back on us* London, Age Concern

Hall, M P (1965) *The Social Services of Modern England* 6th edn, London, Routledge and Kegan Paul

Help the Aged (1999) *Dignity on the Ward* London, Help the Aged

Hinchcliffe, D (1997) 'Bringing down the Berlin Wall?' *ADSS News* October, pp14–17

Jefferys, M (1965) *An Anatomy of Social Welfare Services* London, Michael Joseph

Lewis, J and Glennerster, H (1996) *Implementing the New Community Care* Buckingham, Open University Press

Office for National Statistics (1999) *Social Focus on Older People* London, The Stationery Office

Parry, N and Parry, J (1979) 'Social work, professionalism and the state' in Parry, N, Rustin, M and Satyamurti, C (eds) *Social Work, Welfare and the State* London, Arnold, pp 21–47

Seebohm Report: Seebohm, F (1968) *Report of The Committee on Local Authority and Allied Personal Social Services* London, HMSO, Cmnd. 3703

Sutherland, S (1999) *With Respect to Old Age: a report of the Royal Commission on Long Term Care* London, HMSO

Walton, RG (1975) *Women in Social Work* London, Routledge

Younghusband, E (1959) *Report of the Working Party on Social Workers in the Local Authority Health and Welfare Services* London, HMSO

Chapter 1
The Primary Health Care Interface
Mark Lymbery and Andy Millward

Introduction
This chapter explores the interface between social work and primary health care at a local level. It focuses on three pilot projects within primary health care settings in Nottinghamshire. Two social workers were located on a half-time basis in different general practices, and a full-time social worker was placed in a health centre accommodating several practices. The chapter is based on the evaluation data from the projects.

The data has been analysed from three linked perspectives – structural-organisational, interprofessional and interpersonal (Beattie, 1994; Lymbery, 1999a). The projects have generated particularly valuable material in respect of the first two themes, where they have demonstrated an alternative to the reactive climate that has characterised much community care practice. As we argue, this is in line with the thinking of the Labour Government in developing primary care led health and social services. The integrative nature of the social work role within the projects runs counter to the fragmentation engendered by rigid purchaser–provider splits and presents more positive possibilities for the professional future of social work. The projects have also raised key issues concerning the relative autonomy of social workers when compared to other comparable workers, which lead to tensions regarding management and accountability.

The chapter starts with a summary of the main national policy contexts within which the projects have taken place, paying particular attention to the developing agenda of the Labour administration. It also places the projects in a historical context, by surveying the extensive literature on the connections between social work and primary health care and drawing out key learning points. After discussing the evaluation data for the Nottinghamshire projects, the chapter concludes by considering the distinctive contribution social work can make to primary care, and discusses how social workers can best carry out their roles in this environment.

The policy context
The 1990 NHS and Community Care Act heralded far-reaching changes in the assessment and delivery of social care. It was finally implemented in April 1993 into a turbulent environment of increasing resource constraints imposed by public sector fiscal policy (George and Wilding, 1994), against a background of

rising demand on both health and social services. In general terms, it required that Social Services Departments (SSDs) become managed organisations and adopt a business and market oriented philosophy. As various writers have argued, this created a fertile climate for the 'new managerialism' (Langan and Clarke, 1994; Harris, 1998). The organisational form of SSDs underwent a major shift, with the bureau-professional compromise, characteristic of the post-Seebohm welfare organisation, replaced by an emphasis on managerially dominated priorities – notably the overwhelming need to manage budgets (Hadley and Clough, 1996; Lewis and Glennerster, 1996). For social workers, this changing organisational landscape had an apparently paradoxical effect. On the one hand it gave greater prominence to their work, and challenged the historical domination of social work by childcare priorities. However, this change of focus was accompanied by a transition from a comprehensive professional role into one that is narrower and more fragmented (Sturges, 1996), under the impact of financial imperatives reinforced by highly prescriptive management (Lymbery, 1998b).

Against this background, many in the social care field have welcomed the stress on modernising social services contained in a plethora of guidance and legislative intention by the Labour administration, most fully summarised in the White Paper, *Modernising Social Services* (DoH, 1998c). The welfare policies of the Labour government were unclear on its accession to government; however, the themes that have subsequently emerged – an emphasis on partnership, performance, standards and regulation (Balloch, 1998) – have been emphasised within numerous official publications.

The concept of 'joined up thinking' has been at the heart of policy developments in both central and local government. Although the implications of such an approach for social work are vague, it may be possible to identify social work as a potential contributor within the policy areas of social inclusion, welfare to work, the New Deal for communities and action zones in education, environment and health. In particular, it is possible for social work to play a key role in combating the social reasons for much ill health. However, it is uncommon to find a social worker making substantial contributions to such initiatives unless directly employed in some form of community development capacity. Organisational arrangements within SSDs militate against such inclusive intentions as the assessment imperative and its individualised restrictions dominate the social work agenda.

The White Paper on the future of the health service (DoH, 1997b) heralded an immediate shift in the organisation of primary care commissioning, with the replacement of GP fundholding with primary care groups (PCGs), which became operational in April 1999. The development of PCGs is notable for several reasons:

- It signals a commitment to the centrality of primary care within the NHS, and registers the importance of collaboration and partnership.

- In this spirit, the location of a manager from SSDs on the PCG boards gives scope – albeit limited – for the development of mainstream joint commissioning.

- The delivery and commissioning of primary care are combined within one framework, involving the development of a population framework and needs assessments into aggregated forms for planning purposes.

- It raises questions about the extent to which resources for social care will remain under local authority control, leading to concerns about an increasing 'democratic deficit' in both social and health care.

Although PCGs offer the potential for shifting the power base from hospital to primary and community care, it is important to be cautious about their ability to effect change. The new reforms are politically driven, and are proceeding without robust evidence to inform or guide policy. To that extent, at least, they are as much of an experiment as the system of fundholding that they replaced. There are also a number of practical problems that have affected their introduction. Within local PCGs, early indications suggest that the agenda is dominated by relatively narrow health service considerations, although significant time and energy has been devoted to intra-group understandings. Issues of significance to social services have had less of an impact. The dominance of health service concerns is perhaps not surprising, but a few PCG-board sponsored joint projects with social care elements are no substitute for the development of a commissioning strategy driven by locality and population needs. Bureaucratic demands continue to have a disproportionate impact on board agendas, due in part to the continuing role of the health authority in scrutinising PCG developments. The drive for Primary Care Trust status will now no doubt consume the energies of those in the health community generally, many of whom will have Community Trust backgrounds and will have been involved in partnership initiatives. Paradoxically, their future employment insecurities may well lead to a form of planning blight as new organisational forms restrict the innovation and development that national policy wishes of primary care. (A similar pattern was seen in the round of local government reorganisation through the mid-1990s – see Craig and Manthorpe, 1998).

The National Priorities Guidance 1999/00–2001/02 (DoH, 1998b) failed to meet its stated objective of breaking down barriers between services by restricting the social services lead on interagency working to children's services only. It would also have been useful for the Shared Lead Priorities in Promoting Independence to have contained more of a focus on proposed organisational models of collaborative effort and integration. The potential for collaborative working between health and social care was instead left for exploration in the *Partnership in Action* discussion document (DoH, 1998a), which raised the possibility of pooled budgets, integrated provision and lead commissioning responsibilities. However, the Health Service Circular *Primary Care Groups: taking the next steps* (DoH, 1999b) was notable for its almost complete focus on managerial and clinical issues.

Caution is needed about the implications of collaborative developments for social work, given the historical concern that the occupation could be absorbed into health, and hence lose its distinctive identity (Huntington, 1981). *Partnership in Action* does state that 'major structural change is not the answer' (DoH, 1998a, p. 5), and gives an indication of a willingness to work within – and improve – existing mechanisms for collaboration. By contrast, the Health Select Committee Report (DoH, 1999a) recommended that there should be structural change to merge the different agencies involved in the delivery of primary care. The Government has responded to 30 recommendations of the Select Committee's report (DoH, 1999a) and key points include:

- More performance monitoring and better mechanisms for sharing best practice;
- The development of a national framework for transparent and uniform processes for eligibility criteria;
- A recommendation that professional roles be reviewed and a proposal for more joint training;
- A recommendation that the NHS makes targeted long-term investments in complementary local authority services;
- A recommendation that social services teams should be coterminous with PCG areas;
- A recommendation that pilot projects be established to test ways of integrating health and social services.

The White Paper *Modernising Social Services* (DoH, 1998c) had been trailed for many months, and finally appeared in December 1998. It proposed the establishment of a Social Services Modernisation Fund, which is a clear expression of the Government's emphasis on locally based partnerships; £650 million has been made available over three years to help foster such arrangements. However, in a continuation of what has been a depressing litany within social services, there continue to be doubts about the adequacy of funding. Indeed, the Prevention Grant which was intended as a mechanism to ensure authorities consider their preventative responsibilities in responding to need and delivering services, is only for a three-year period. Although the aspiration is for developments under its banner to be absorbed into mainstream budgets, the objective is naïve without considerable realignment of other resources, the home care service being a prime example.

In addition, the increasingly performance driven climate is not likely to be helpful to developmental initiatives. The development of BEST VALUE initiatives in local government was meant to signal a break with the Conservative past, while improving the overall quality of all local government services. However, BEST VALUE is still heavily dependent on the establishment of performance targets, exemplified by the Performance Assessment Framework (DoH, 1999c); it also signifies an intention to compare authorities, and to hold individual departments to account for poor performance. The publication of national league tables in November 1999 demonstrated the varied nature of performance around the country and showed that the New Labour Government was serious in its commitment to root out poor practice. Many Directors of Social Services were alarmed at their inclusion in the poor performance category, especially when they had been advised that there would be no 'naming and shaming' element to their publication (Community Care, 1999). Directors were also concerned at the one-dimensional aspect of the information collated and suggested that much data was of insufficient quality to justify the sweeping judgements that resulted. Only two out of fifty indicators regarding adults and older people have an interagency component, in the areas of emergency admissions of older people (A5) and delayed discharge (D51). It would have been more appropriate to the development of integrated health and social care systems to have recognised indicators such as the number of joint initiatives and cross-working arrangements than the narrow indicators prescribed.

However, the emphasis within the Performance Assessment Framework clearly connects to postmodern notions of 'performativity' (see Howe, 1994), where practice becomes task-orientated, performance related, quantifiable, measurable and hence easier to control (Everitt, 1996). In the process, professional values of empathy and service become less important, and may even be seen as obstacles to efficient performance according to the set criteria. This could have a significant effect on the preventative and developmental possibilities of social work in primary health care (noted below), and force SSDs into even more reactive and defensive forms of practice.

The history of social work in primary health care

Recent years have seen a plethora of published papers and reports on the subject of social work in primary health care settings (see, for example, McIntosh and Bennett-Emslie, 1993; Pithouse and Butler, 1994; Cumella, le Mesurier and Tomlin, 1996; Hardy, Leedham, and Wistow, 1996; Hudson *et al.*, 1997; Simic, 1997; Lymbery, 1998a; Russell Hodgson, 1998; Hudson, 1999a and 1999b). Several reports have also summarised core issues regarding the development of social work and primary care (CAIPE, 1996; Poxton, 1999a and 1999b). As the previous chapter makes clear, the emphasis on community care to be provided in partnership by different agencies has fostered this interest. However, a substantial literature on social work and general practice was already in existence (see, for example, Collins, 1965; Forman and Fairbairn, 1968; Goldberg and Neill, 1972; Huntington, 1981; Clare and Corney, 1982; Butrym and Horder, 1983; Rushton and Davies, 1984; Cairns Smith, 1989). On the basis that some understanding of historical developments should inform current practice, this chapter will outline the main contributions to the history of social work in general practice.

The main reasons why social work was first established in primary health care included the lack of unity that characterised social services of the time and the division between medical and social care (Collins, 1965). The work of the Younghusband Committee (Younghusband, 1959) provided a significant impetus, noting the potential of social work to promote preventative and multi-disciplinary working within general practice. The medical profession voiced a growing recognition that it was 'impossible to practise domiciliary medicine without involvement in social and emotional problems' (Forman and Fairbairn, 1968, p.5). It was argued that this implied the creation of multi-skilled health and social care teams to provide a coordinated response to need (Goldberg and Neill, 1972), although this concept developed less quickly than had originally been envisaged (Dedman, 1996).

The Seebohm Report (1968, para. 690) acknowledged that cooperation between social workers and doctors was generally poor. From this starting point, it gave unequivocal support to the principle of improving collaboration between doctors and social workers:

> Survey after survey has shown that many family doctors do not seek
> help from social workers nor use social services that are available:
> they often do not know about them, or do not understand or value them
> . . . Realistic attempts at prevention in the social field, whether in

detecting early trouble or intervening at times of crisis . . . will often have to be based on family practice and organised as a joint effort of doctors and social workers. General practice today is in touch with a higher proportion of those who are in difficulties than any of the other social services and it needs the full support of them all. (Seebohm Report, 1968, para. 692)

The report argued that effective teamwork between general practitioners and social services was vital (para. 699) and referred approvingly to the experiments that were in progress (Collins, 1965; Forman and Fairbairn, 1968).

Where arrangements were made to place social workers within general practice, the positive nature of the experiences was evident. For example, Goldberg and Neill (1972) concluded that the location of a social worker within the health centre led to a closer focus on the links between medical and social needs, and helped to promote a more flexible and imaginative response. They also highlighted the potential of GP-attached social workers to provide a proactive service for older people. Forman and Fairbairn (1968) noted that the doctors, health visitors and social worker involved in their project were equally enthusiastic about its results. Collins (1965) included a range of comments from patients that indicates that they were (by and large) positive about the service they received. Numerous writers commented that the location of social workers within general practice appeared to draw a wider range of people into social services (Corney, 1980; Corney and Bowen, 1982; Sheppard, 1983; Cairns Smith, 1989).

However, some criticisms were evident amongst the general enthusiasm. For example, Collins (1965) noted that there were insufficient social workers to staff attachments to all health centres. She also expressed concern about the willingness of some doctors to value the social components of health care, and implied that what works on an exceptional level may not be appropriate when applied on a more systematic basis. Goldberg and Neill (1972) also questioned the readiness of some GPs to accept a more social orientation, and commented that social services organisations may have more pressing priorities than the establishment of widespread attachments to general practice. Many of these points have considerable contemporary resonance.

The 1970s saw a formal separation between health and social services, with the reorganisation of the NHS and the creation of local authority social services departments (SSDs) (Hugman, 1995), which emphasised the distinctions between the two. However, by this time the principle of collaborative working had been established (Jefferys, 1995); this was reaffirmed in the National Health Service Reorganisation Act of 1973. In addition, the Otton Report

(1974) on social work support for the health service argued that the work of doctors and social workers was complementary, and that effective collaboration between the two would improve the level of preventive work (para. 49). The Report went so far as to recommend that 'all new health centres will be designed to include accommodation for the use of social workers' (para. 45).

However, as Osborn (1996) reported, there was only sporadic and unsystematic development of the theme in the 1970s and 1980s. In some areas interest was sustained in the development of social work services within general practice, and numerous schemes were started in the 1970s, particularly in response to the advent of pump-priming money through joint finance in 1976 (Rushton and Davies, 1984). Indeed, it was estimated that half of SSDs contained one or more such project in the late 1970s (Gough and Scott, 1979, cited in Rushton and Davies, 1984). The literature on the subject still reported such schemes as success stories (Graham and Sher, 1976; Rushton and Briscoe, 1981), but also examined in more detail the areas of unease identified in earlier studies.

For example, Huntington (1981) concluded that core differences between doctors and social workers – status, income, training, ideology, location and distribution – may predict major problems in working together as equal partners. Similarly, Bruce (1980) averred that the unequal professional status of doctors and social workers would tend to lead to a dominant – dependent relationship between the two, with a necessary impact on collaborative working. Bywaters (1986) argued that a true collaboration between social work and the medical profession meant that there should be no unconditional acceptance of medical dominance, but that it should be predicated on the promotion of a social model of health. While accepting the existence of inequalities between the key occupational groups within primary health care, Dingwall (1982) suggested that the relationship between these professions could lead to a struggle for power and control, through a process of what he termed 'occupational boundary maintenance'. However, Ratoff (1973) contended that there was little evidence of such role conflict when multidisciplinary teams were working well.

Ratoff, Rose and Smith (1974) noted the problems that could be created by the fundamentally different approaches of GPs and social workers. They also commented on the impact of variations in the methods and tempo of their work, the complex decision-making processes required within SSDs and issues such as authority and accountability. By contrast, Dalley (1989) drew attention to a process which she termed 'tribal allegiance', where different occupational groups may develop similar perspectives on problems, irrespective of their professional backgrounds. In the light of the power imbalances between GPs and social workers, an effect of this could be that the social worker loses a sense of the specific contribution of the social work discipline to the interprofessional setting. Rushton and Davies (1984) pointed to the fact that, in such circumstances, it is tempting for social workers to collude with dominant medical perspectives and hence lose their professional integrity.

Corney (1980) concluded that a range of factors affected the success of social work attachment schemes. It is worth citing these in detail, since they prefigure some of the conclusions we have reached in the Nottinghamshire study (Lymbery, 1998a; Lymbery and Millward, 1998). Five specific issues are listed by Corney:

- The suitability of the facilities (separate room, telephone facilities, and so on) within the practice for the social worker, and the time s/he spentat the site. In general, Corney felt that where a social worker was permanently located within the practice better informal contacts would be established, leading to more productive working relation ships. While she acknowledged that liaison schemes could bring about benefits, she concluded that these would be slower to develop, and more limited in value.

- The proportion of the caseload managed directly by the social worker, and adequate time to manage the work. She concluded that there were advantages if the social worker was able to manage the full caseload, although she acknowledged the professional isolation that might be a consequence of this.

- The organisation of the practice and the nature of the key personalities involved. Corney argued that the practice must have a genuine commitment to the primary care team and to social models of health care, and a desire to make the team effective. She identified the attitudes of GPs as being central to this, alongside the maturity and competence of the social worker.

- Location of the social worker within the broader context of a health centre would carry additional benefits, particularly as it would help to draw other professionals – notably community nurses – into the arrangement.

- The importance of good preliminary discussion with the social services department, and effective continuing liaison.

It is interesting that there were relatively few published papers on social work in general practice in the 1980s, after the profusion of the 1970s. However, the theme was rediscovered following the publication of the community care White Paper (DoH, 1989, para. 4.11–4.18), which called for closer cooperation between SSDs and GPs. This was further expanded in the subsequent Policy Guidance, which stated that 'GPs will wish to make a full contribution to assessment' (DoH, 1990, para. 3.47), in recognition of the close links between health and social care. As a result, there was increased interest in the subject through the 1990s, as the number of published papers bears testimony (McIntosh and Bennett-Emslie, 1993; Pithouse and Butler, 1994; Cumella *et al.*, 1996; Hardy *et al.*, 1996; Hudson *et al.*, 1997; Lymbery, 1998a). This links to the general increase in attention given to interprofessional working, which is usefully summarised by Hudson (1999a and 1999b).

The social and economic climate within which social work is practised has changed massively since the first wave of attachment schemes (see Langan, 1993), particularly in community care. The introduction of care management has limited the horizons of social work, and laid particular emphasis on needs-led assessment followed by the establishment of packages of care (Lymbery, 1998b). This has led to reduced emphasis on the therapeutic aspect of social work, which had been valued by many previous commentators (Graham and Sher, 1976; Corney and Briscoe, 1977; Rushton and Briscoe, 1981). Indeed, Ratoff (1973) had identified therapeutic work as one of the four key functions of a social worker in general practice, alongside assessment, liaison and education. Even though the nature of the social work task has changed, and therapeutic work is unlikely to occupy the bulk of a social worker's time, many writers still argue that care management practice is sensibly located within primary health care settings (see McIntosh and Bennett-Emslie, 1993).

Recent evaluations of social work in primary health care continue to demonstrate positive results. For example, Hardy *et al.*, (1996) found that it helped to improve professional collaboration and alleviate mutual suspicion. Cumella *et al.*, (1996) concluded that such arrangements improved the quality of cooperative working between the various parties, and identified three specific areas of improvement – liaison, access to services and productivity. Russell Hodgson (1998) echoed the final point. However, in some evaluations the organisational benefits to health have outweighed those to social services (see Challis and Pearson, 1993), leading to concerns that the social worker is still acting as a 'handmaiden' (Huntington, 1981) to the dominant medical profession. As Hudson (1999a) has commented, the resources to which a social worker has access are the primary benefits to the rest of the primary care team, over and above any counselling work with which the social worker might be engaged.

Evidence from the King's Fund Joint Commissioning Project (Poxton 1999a and 1999b) offered insights into the problems that have hindered successful progress of primary health and social care partnerships. It noted that joint working is not widespread and relies heavily on the inclinations of the few. Confusion was frequently found between the terms 'joint working' and 'joint commissioning' – this lack of conceptual clarity inhibiting better integrated care for both individual users and the wider population. It appears that joint commissioning failed to flourish particularly when based around particular GP practices or a group of practices. Users and carers were not often involved in projects, perhaps echoing the fragile nature of the professional partnerships. Weak vertical links between decisions made at practice, locality and strategic levels were a feature of most joint commissioning pilots. The SSI publication *Of Primary Importance* (DoH, 1999d) examined the links of eight social services departments with primary health services for older people. Their findings largely confirmed the concerns expressed above. This accepted that there has been a development of a broad range of small-scale partnerships, demonstrating a rich mixture of operational models. However, the report identified a general lack of joint strategic and operational activity between social services departments and primary health services.

From the literature, it is possible to identify the benefits and potential disadvantages of the model of social worker attachments to general practice. Broadly speaking, the benefits include the following:

- Ease of access to social services through the accessibility of doctors' surgeries
- Reduced likelihood that such services will be perceived as stigmatising
- Improved mutual respect, communication and cooperation between professions
- Better, more holistic, needs-led assessments
- More effective teamwork
- A swifter response to need

The potential problems are as follows:

- Accountability issues
- Professional struggles over 'occupational boundary maintenance'
- Differences in ideology and value systems between professions
- The professional isolation of the social worker
- Conflict between incompatible goals of SSD and the general practice

- Ineffective managerial support for the social worker
- Role confusion for the social worker.

However, as Higgins (1994) pointed out, the problems are not insuperable. Several writers have commented on the importance of proper planning and coordination of projects (Rushton and Davies, 1984; Hardy *et al.*, 1996). Others (Gregson, Cartlidge and Bond, 1991; Pithouse and Butler, 1994; CAIPE, 1996; Lymbery, 1998a) have identified a range of practical steps – greater clarity of the purposes of collaboration, clear management and direction of the project, increased understanding of each other's roles, ensuring commitment to the overall goals, shared recording systems, regular meetings – which can improve the quality of joint working. The following factors characterised those projects which appear to have secured successful outcomes:

- Detailed planning and preparation of all involved staff
- Active co-ordination, management, leadership of the project
- Availability of adequate resources for the project
- Goodwill from all parties within the project
- Responsiveness to local circumstances
- The personal maturity of key participants (particularly the social worker)
- Clarity about the roles and functions of all people involved in the project
- The full commitment of all parties.

  (Material adapted from Bruce, 1980; Rushton and Davies, 1984; Gregson *et al.*, 1991; Challis and Pearson, 1993; Pithouse and Butler, 1994; Cumella *et al.*, 1996; Hardy *et al.*, 1996; Hudson *et al.*, 1997; Lymbery, 1998a.)

In summary, most of what has been written is positive, albeit aware of the potential pitfalls. We next outline the contribution that the research within Nottinghamshire makes to the existing evidence, starting with a description of the projects, leading to a summary of the key factors to have emerged from their evaluation.

The Nottinghamshire projects: setting the scene
Here we describe the projects and the objectives that were agreed for them, and outline the research methods that were used in their evaluation. The projects originated in Nottinghamshire in 1996, following two separate sets

of negotiation between health and social services regarding ways to increase the level of cooperative working between social workers, doctors and community nurses. Nottinghamshire is a mixed urban and rural area, with a total population of just over one million people. Around 300,000 people live in the city of Nottingham, which is located in the south of the county. At the start of the project one SSD covered the entire county. In April 1998 a new SSD was established for Nottingham City as a result of the process of local government reorganisation, thereby reducing the size of the county SSD; the implications of this will be discussed shortly. There are two health authorities. North Nottinghamshire Health Authority covers the north and east of the county and serves a population of approximately 400,000 people. Nottingham Health Authority covers the city and its immediate suburbs (a population of around 600,000 people). All three projects were located within the Nottingham Health Authority, two within the city of Nottingham, and one within the county. The projects were initially funded for two years from joint finance, and became operational in October 1996. Additional money was found to extend their life by a further six months, so that they came to an end in April 1999.

Different operational arrangements governed the projects, a legacy of the separate negotiations that had brought them into being. One social worker worked initially on a half-time basis within a large group practice (serving approximately 11,000 people) in a suburban area to the west of the city (subsequently referred to as Project 1); after 18 months this post was converted to full-time in acknowledgement of the high caseload. The second social worker worked on a half-time basis within a smaller practice (serving approximately 6,000 people) in the north of the city (subsequently referred to as Project 2). The third social worker was based full-time in an inner-city health centre (subsequently referred to as Project 3) housing three separate practices, and serving a very mixed population of around 30,000, including a high proportion of people from ethnic minorities, as well as large numbers of transient students. The first two posts were specifically linked to GPs; the third post contained the added dimension of closer working links with community or district nurses, with whom the social worker shared an office. All three projects followed the model of 'co-location' (Hardy *et al.*, 1996), with the social workers physically situated in the health care setting, away from the assessment and care management teams (ACMTs) that provided the standard community care service from social services offices. All three social workers had a general remit for adult services; the bulk of their work was with older people.

The objectives of the projects were as follows:

1. To enable people with health and social care needs and their carers to have a single point of access to services.

2. To provide a convenient local service for people with health and social care needs and their carers.

3. To enable primary health care staff to identify with a named member of the social services staff.

4. To improve the appropriateness of referral and the accuracy and relevance of information communicated between primary health care and social services staff.

5. To improve communication between primary health care and social services staff through the sharing of information, including access to each other's records.

6. To improve response times in social services activity, from referral to allocation, assessment start, completion of assessment and the establishment of services.

7. To improve the degree and quality of joint working between health and social services staff in assessment and the establishment and management of services.

8. To improve interagency pre-admission and discharge planning for hospital patients.

9. To investigate the reasons for perceived failures in hospital discharge affecting the practice and to make recommendations for action.

10. To explore opportunities for early preventative help for patients of the practice.

11. To improve the awareness and usage of the wider network of statutory and nonstatutory resources available for people with health and social care needs and their carers.

In organising the evaluation strategy we followed the line that the best approach is one that 'matches research methods to the evaluation questions being asked' (Patton, 1980: p.17). In addition, the small scale of the projects and the limited budget available for evaluation effectively dictated both what was, and was not, possible. It was decided that the pursuit of outcome-based research would not be feasible, and the priority was to analyse the structures, processes and attitudes (Gregson *et al.*, 1991) to collaborative work in the three projects. The most important research task was therefore to understand the experiences of the project from the perspective of the key participants (Patton, 1978). A core method for seeking such perceptions was through semi-structured interviews (Marshall and Rossman, 1989); these were conducted with participants on a systematic basis at the start, the middle and the end of the project. In total 45 interviews – of social workers, GPs, community nurses, social services managers and practice administrative staff – were carried out over the life of the project. Naturally, these interviews produced data which was concerned with 'individuals' own accounts of their attitudes, motivations and behaviour' (Hakim, 1987, p.26), and which produced descriptive and interpretative reports of their experiences.

We also took the view that it was important to acquire data from a range of other sources, using a variant of 'administrative anthropology' advocated by Lewis and Glennerster (1996). This involved a close engagement with the project, using a combination of both 'soft' interview data and 'hard' data generated through policy documents and computer systems. The social workers provided a number of case studies to reflect the distinctive nature of their practice. In addition, we were both members of the Steering Group, which met on a quarterly basis through the life of the projects. The social workers and their line managers also met with us on a quarterly basis. Information acquired from both sets of meetings was used in the evaluation process; the meetings also gave an opportunity to check progress on a regular basis. Taken overall, the different sources of information helped with the process of 'validity checking' (Marshall and Rossman, 1989) of all the data collected.

The Nottinghamshire projects: evaluation
The purpose of this part of the chapter is to give an overall impression of the projects' progress. It draws upon Beattie's (1994) distinction between the different levels of analysis that should be applied to interprofessional work. He identified three particular strands of thought:

- 'Disparities in organisational arrangements', in which he included issues such as autonomy, accountability, pay, management and planning. We have termed this the 'structural-organisational' level.

- 'Competing professional rationales', which derives from the mixture of social and professional ideologies of the different groups. We have labelled this as the 'interprofessional' level.

- 'Psychodynamics of interpersonal relations', which examines the personal interaction of individuals. We have termed this the 'interpersonal' level.

Beattie argued that full understanding is gained through an analysis of how the different levels interact. We have applied this framework in previous papers (Lymbery, 1998a; Lymbery and Millward, 1998); it is similar to the approach taken by Hudson *et al*. (1997).

We start with some general observations on the success of the projects. The experience of locating a social worker within primary health care settings was strongly valued by most of the parties involved, a conclusion which holds for all three settings. The highest levels of enthusiasm came from the social workers, as well as all the health personnel interviewed. Where concerns were raised, these were more likely to be from social services managers who had the responsibility to ensure that the project was effectively coordinated, and had the responsibility to plan for its succession. Even here, the general sense conveyed was that the projects had met the bulk of their objectives and had proved to be successful in their own terms. Local government reorganisation had a considerable impact on the project, notably in the high turnover of middle management staff: Project 1 had particular problems with lack of continuity at this level. In addition, local government reorganisation proved in general to have been an unsettling experience and not one conducive to seeing through developmental opportunities (see Craig and Manthorpe, 1998, for a broader discussion of this).

In terms of the specific objectives, the evaluation concluded that there was evidence for the achievement of most of them, if not quite all. The following paragraphs briefly explain the extent to which each objective was met.

1. As knowledge about the role of the social worker increased within the practice population, so too did the rate of referral. An examination of the source of referrals is illuminating: in all three projects the vast majority came direct from the practice rather than through the standard duty system. In effect, therefore, the social workers operated their own duty systems. The sources of referral in Project 3 make interesting reading, with over half the referrals (93/176) coming from a range of community nurses – district nurses, health visitors, community psychiatric nurses. This is a much higher figure than is evident at either of the other two projects, which had a more traditional focus on links with the GPs. The disparity appears to be a facet of the direct communication possible between the social worker and community nurses at Project 3.

2. The presence of a social worker in a health care setting is more convenient for potential service users than the normal social services duty system. There was evidence that the projects actively enabled some sections of the community to secure access to social services. For example, an

analysis of the computer mainframe data indicated that the take-up of services by people from ethnic minorities at Project 3 was particularly striking in comparison with the assessment and care management teams which covered a similar geographic area. One-third of the referrals to the social worker in Project 3 were from ethnic minorities, particularly from Muslim women. This is not only a much higher rate of such referrals than would come to ordinary social workers in the team, it is also higher than the percentage managed by the specialist social worker for ethnic minorities in the team. This suggests that access to social services through a GP was less stigmatising than normal routes, supporting earlier research (Rushton and Briscoe, 1981).

3.   All staff within the primary health care team were satisfied with the ease of access to a social worker, contrasting this favourably with the situation which prevailed before the projects began. One respondent noted that it was much easier to communicate with the social worker, and that this helped improve levels of coordination; GPs found this aspect of the project to have been particularly valuable.

4.   Referrals to the social workers were seen as largely appropriate, and that this improved as the project became more established. For GPs, one of the key benefits was that the modes of referral were mostly verbal – this clearly suited their needs, and enabled them to have an easier route of access into social services. The district nurses at Project 3 reported a similar improvement.

5.   There was more sharing of information within the project than had been the norm previously. For example, social workers had ready access to medical records. One social worker stated that she 'felt more informed' about medical and health matters generally, thereby improving her professional judgements. Several respondents spoke of the improved levels of trust between different disciplines, which led to more cooperative working.

6.   It was commonly believed, particularly by health services personnel, that social services' response times within the project were better than the norm, even in the two situations where a single part-time worker carried out the work. (However, there was no hard data to confirm these impressions.) In these circumstances, medical personnel were happy to wait for the social worker's return for the cases to be seen, and were perhaps more flexible in that respect than they would otherwise have been.

7.   The first part of this objective was achieved, in that all respondents directly involved in the project were convinced that joint working had been enhanced. At Project 3 there was a particular emphasis on the development of joint work between the social worker and district nurses. Elsewhere the emphasis was more on links between social workers and GPs; a relatively small amount of joint visiting was described, although all parties actively involved in day-to-day work commented that there was a higher level of consultation over work. As an analysis of case files indicated, joint working did extend beyond the assessment phase into the management of services, and required active processes of monitoring and review.

8&9. These two objectives were less systematically addressed than the other nine. Each setting reported few occasions where there were failed or unsafe discharges. Therefore, although all three social workers considered these issues, at least in part, insufficient information for future planning was forthcoming. There was case study evidence of the value of a social worker providing continuity of support both before and after hospital admission. However, the evaluation provides insufficient evidence to enable an informed judgement whether locating of social workers within primary health care settings can make a marked difference in respect of safe discharge and pre-admission discharge planning.

10. Only limited preventative and developmental work was accomplished, with the full-time social worker at Project 3 being able to achieve most in this respect. The lack of progress in the other two settings was more a function of workload than any other factor. As previous research has indicated (Corney and Bowen, 1982), the location of a social worker within primary health care settings widened access to social services; this had the unintended consequence of increasing the pressure of work on the already hard-stretched SSD. From the limited evidence of Project 3, the location of a social worker within a primary health care setting did help to facilitate preventative work. In general, all social workers were involved in cases at an earlier level, and dealt with more people with lower levels of need. However, the projects did not last for a sufficient length of time to judge whether early social work involvement helped to prevent a rapid decline in people's health.

11. While there was little direct evidence that this objective was met, the projects appeared to facilitate a greater level of awareness of the role of social services. That workloads were higher than anticipated testifies to this, as does the fact that the take-up of services from ethnic minorities

was much higher in Project 3.The work pattern of the social worker within Project 1 is an interesting example of the first point. In the first two years, 18 months of which were part-time, this practitioner dealt with 157 referrals, as against 176 for the full-time worker at Project 3. This was both a higher referral rate than anticipated, and a much heavier workload than was the norm within the assessment and care management teams. Part of this may be attributed to the fact that the social workers accepted work of a type that would otherwise be allocated to staff at a lower level. However, it seems probable that locating a social worker within primary health care does serve to increase take-up of services, as hypothesised in the objectives.

Using Beattie's typology (1994), the benefits of the project are listed in Table 1.1

Table 1.1   Benefits of the project

Structural/ organisational	Professional/ cultural	Interpersonal
• Improved care outcomes • Better coordination of services • Continuity within care services • Quicker response times • Social services more accessible to service users	• Improved communication and working relationships • Health care staff having more insight into social work role • More autonomy/ flexibility in the social work role • The opportunity to engage in developmental work	• More job satisfaction • Greater levels of personal collaboration over the content of work

The main areas of criticism were identified as follows:

Table 1.2   Criticisms of the project

Structural/ organisational	Professional/ cultural	Inter-personal
• Lack of integration of projects into the work of ACMTs • The social workers carried a high workload, leading to a more reactive than anticipated form of practice • Issues regarding management, supervision and accountability • Experienced social workers carrying out low level tasks • Equity issues, by comparison with normal ACMT provision • Gains were felt more by health; problems more by social services	• Some degree of professional isolation for the social workers	• Some degree of personal isolation for the social workers

For the majority of respondents the advantages of the project clearly outweighed the problems. In Project 1, a GP commented that the project had provided an 'ideal' service. In Project 3, a district nurse described the project has having provided a 'superb, brilliant service'. In Project 2, a GP stated that she 'did not wish to return to the previous system'. The social workers themselves were equally enthusiastic about the projects, with consistent themes underpinning their perspectives. The social worker in Project 1 described it as 'brilliant', and that it was 'what social work should be', while the worker in Project 2 felt that were great improvements in continuity of care and communication. The social worker in Project 3 particularly valued the developmental work she had been able to initiate, and characterised the experience as having been personally and professionally very positive. All three social workers had valued the autonomy, flexibility and level of responsibility that characterised the role, and felt that the quality of multidisciplinary working had improved the service provided.

If one relates the findings to the existing research evidence (see p.21), this perspective is borne out. All of the benefits have been fully evidenced, while not all the disadvantages have been similarly evident. For example, there were few problems around interprofessional working, where the personal maturity and skill of the social workers was a positive influence on the direction of the projects. However, it is worth noting that the overwhelming balance of negative comments relates to structural and organisational factors; while there were potential problems around professional/cultural and interpersonal areas, these were not experienced to any significant degree in the projects. We would judge that a key reason for the successful outcome is that the prerequisites for a successful project (see p.22) had been considered in advance (Lymbery, 1998a) and were in evidence in its operation.

The more critical voices tended to be those of social services managers. For example, one indicated that the gains to the SSD were not clear-cut, and that the projects had a limited impact on the wider organisation. This respondent also felt that while the unresolved issues around autonomy and accountability were manageable within the context of the project, they could create a major problem if it were 'rolled out'. There was a general concern that success in a project did not necessarily mean that success in a wider context could be guaranteed; the fact that so many of the critical issues are located within the structural/organisational level is testimony to the extent of this concern. The following section will pursue further the implications of some of these points.

The future of social work in primary health care
The main purposes of this section are:
- To identify the main points that need to be clarified if the model of social worker co-location in primary health care is to be more widely developed.

- To reflect on the extent to which closer links between social work and primary health care fit within the Government's policy framework.

31

- To consider the extent to which a primary health care location may provide an opportunity for the enhancement of social work practice in the context of community care.

Developing co-location as an organisational model

Given the positive evaluations that have characterised social work in primary health care over the past 35 years, it is interesting that social workers who are physically located within general practice are still the exception rather than the rule. We believe that this might be due to the fact that successful pilot projects may not be easily transferred into mainstream SSD work. There are two main reasons for this:

- Pilot projects enjoy favourable status, and are set up with every chance of success. However, when translated into more standard forms, it is possible that problems that either did not emerge or were discounted have a greater impact.

- Insufficient attention may have been given to the problems that have emerged, perhaps because their significance was not recognised.

Allied to the above two points is the separate issue that pilot or demonstration projects are much more likely to be fully evaluated, and therefore are the ones that dominate the literature. It is much less likely that the reasons underpinning failure will be fully explored. However, there are a number of other factors that affect the issue. Those cited draw substantially on the work of Hudson *et al.*, (1997), and were further developed through the process of evaluation.

Accountability or autonomy?

The social workers particularly valued the level of flexibility inherent in the project, and their separation from the routine work of district based assessment and care management teams; none of them expressed an interest in working as a social worker within the ACMT environment. This flexibility and relative autonomy ensured that they functioned in a way that was most helpful to other primary health care staff. The social workers appreciated the fact that they had a greater level of autonomy than their ACMT colleagues, and substantially organised their own work, which led to a reconceptualisation of the relationship between social worker and team manager. Although autonomy and accountability did not emerge as major problems for the project, if the bulk of adult services were organised in this way some key issues would need to be considered:

- How should the work of social workers be managed? As things currently stand, social workers' practice is more directly controlled than is the norm for similar professionals within the health service (for example, district nurses). There are currently no objective national criteria that govern the work of all social workers, unlike district nurses or GPs, although the creation of a General Social Care Council will change this (DoH, 1998b). Is it reasonable to assume that experienced social workers could operate successfully with a less hands-on form of management in community care?

● What should be expected as standards of performance by social workers? To what extent do they deliver on these expectations? This clearly has a bearing on social work in the ACMT structure, where standards of practice are described as variable. Should work of the quality identified by the projects not be expected of all social workers, given that social workers readily claim professional status? What should be contained in the professional role of the social worker?

Professional isolation

As we have identified, much literature focuses on professional isolation, where an individual is located apart from managerial, professional and peer support. Although this was not reported as a problem in the projects, the social workers only spent two and a half years in the role; had the evaluation have taken place after five years or more, would the social work role still have been carried out so effectively? A prolonged separation from sources of professional support is more likely to have deleterious consequences.

Location of budgets

The social workers had to secure access to social services budgets through normal procedures, with the exception of a small amount of money that was made directly available in Project 3, which was found to have been very useful. It could be argued that flexibility and speed of response would be enhanced if the social worker had control over certain limited forms of budgetary expenditure. If so, to what extent should this be developed, and what are the practical implications of such a policy?

The type of work carried out, and the appropriate form of staffing

The project social workers took a wider range of work than would normally be the case for a level 3 social worker, given that they took most referrals of whatever type from each practice. This is evidenced by comparative data, which demonstrated that while the social workers at Projects 1 and 2 accepted a greater volume of work than their peers in the ACMTs, much of it was at a level that might otherwise have been allocated to an unqualified member of staff. Both of these points strengthen the case for also locating different social services staff within the primary health care setting, as this would increase the diversity of assessment response, and ease access to, for example, home care and occupational therapy. The argument for such diversity is simply that, if the location of a social worker in a health setting makes sense, then so does the location of other social services personnel who work closely with primary health care personnel.

Links to general practice or to primary health care teams?
The separate nature of the projects allowed for an evaluation of the effectiveness of different models – on the one hand, the principal links were to GPs, while on the other they also encompassed the district nurse team. The latter approach added a dimension that has not been present in the other two practices, and facilitated closer integration with the wider primary health care teams, even across three different practices served by the project, and gave an added value to the social worker role. This reinforces the finding of Corney (1980), cited earlier.

Challenges to social services thinking
In many ways, this is the most significant of the issues discussed. Locating social workers within primary health care settings, with the levels of flexibility that they need to be given, runs counter to much current practice within SSDs. This can be seen in three forms:

- First, it means giving social workers more power to make decisions on the spot; in effect, it means returning power from managers to professionals, hence reversing the direction of much community care policy (Harris, 1998). With the financial imperatives of community care continuing to dominate the social services agenda, there is little sign of this occurring.

- The second challenge lies in its explicitly integrative approach, which runs counter to the more formal separation of purchasing and providing which characterised much community care policy on the national level. However, as we have noted earlier, it is very much in tune with government thinking on the development of partnerships between social and health care (DoH, 1998a).

- The third lies in the preventative and developmental goals of the project, which establishes a conflict between the increasingly high-intensity nature of social work, affected by stringent eligibility criteria, and the earlier intervention and lower intensity need addressed by the project. This is given added focus by research that indicates how valuable older people find lower levels of support, which can help enhance people's quality of life and help them maintain their independence (Clark, Dyer and Horwood, 1998) and opens up a debate about the organisation of social services for adults in a time of economic constraint (Simic, 1997).

Social work and primary health care: policy directions

As Balloch (1998) has suggested, although there are continuities between the social services policies of the Conservative and Labour administrations, there are also marked differences. A comparison between the two parties' White Papers on the future of social services makes this point. The Conservative vision (DoH, 1997a) was of a residual public social services function; the core role being to support informal caring networks, and to arrange for publicly funded care only when such networks failed. The White Paper argued that social services should retreat further from their role as direct service providers, with increasing amounts of care expected to be within the independent sector. The explicit reason for this was to reduce costs, and this approach constituted a further privatisation of adult services (Balloch, 1998). There was also considerable emphasis on regulation, with a proposal that inspection functions for residential care should be transferred into newly created statutory bodies separate from SSDs.

While it could be argued that since the Conservatives were poised for a massive defeat in the 1997 general election they had little hope of putting this White Paper into legislative form, it is important for the signal it gave concerning their beliefs about the organisation of social services. Certainly, there was a shift in rhetoric when the Labour Government's White Paper was published (DoH, 1998b); instead of business-derived language, there was an emphasis on concepts like modernisation, standards and partnership. It highlighted the need for services that will promote independence, for the development of partnerships between social services and health (and other agencies), for fairness and consistency both in terms of access to services and in the inspection of services, for more effective protection of vulnerable people, and for clearer standards of performance and more effective arrangements for education and training. The White Paper implied, although did not state, that it represented a break with the recent past; however, it did not seek substantially to alter several key elements of past Conservative policy – notably the emphasis on audit and regulation, and a preoccupation with maintaining tight fiscal controls. Indeed, the development of BEST VALUE has clearly perpetuated these preoccupations (DETR, 1998).

This section will focus on two important developments – the creation of PCGs and the implications of the concept of 'partnership' in health and social care. There are two linked ways in which social work can contribute to these policies. The first is as a core player in the development of primary care groups. The second is in making a reality of the rhetoric of partnership. In respect of PCGs, two of their core functions are particularly interesting from the social work perspective (DoH, 1997b, para. 5.9, p.34):

- The better integration of primary and community health services, and closer working with social services on the planning and delivery of such services.

- The development of primary care through the encouragement of joint working and the sharing of skills.

As far as the organisation of PCGs is concerned, the dominant occupational voice represented on the boards is that of GPs, reflecting their historical hegemony within primary care. However, there are also representatives from community nursing and social services, and there is, in some localities at least, a desire to explore new forms of organisation to facilitate shared working. The model of social worker co-location has already been explored within the three city PCGs within Nottingham Health Authority, building on the success of the pilot projects described earlier. Plans were agreed for expenditure from the Social Services 1999/2000 Partnership Grant for the permanent establishment of two social workers per PCG and a full-time equivalent operations manager. The social workers are now sited in health centres to enable collaborative working, and to facilitate the extension of adult social services into primary care across the city. The appointment of the operations manager appropriately recognises the seniority necessary to work across organisational and professional boundaries in a way that should favour the development of an integrated health and social care service. The absence of a team manager raises interesting questions for the social workers around the issues of autonomy and accountability already discussed.

It is hoped that the extension of the model will achieve the following benefits:

- Improve cooperation between the different professionals involved in the delivery of primary health and social care.

- Provide a more integrated response to need, especially in respect of older people, who are the largest single group of users of both health and social services.

- Provide a more accessible, less stigmatising point of access to social services.

- Enable a more holistic, preventative response to health and social care needs.

As has been demonstrated, locating social workers within primary health care settings can achieve these goals. In addition, this should help to move health and social services into a more genuine mode of partnership. The above goals emphasise an integrated response to need, and help to make a reality of the

Government's hope that PCGs will 'provide unique opportunities for community health services, primary care and social services to co-ordinate the care they provide' (DoH, 1998a, para. 3.10, p.15). In addition, when properly organised and managed, social worker co-location will ensure that the factors needed to sustain effective collaboration between primary health and social services – including better understanding of each other's roles, regular face-to-face contact, shared information and knowledge and so on (CAIPE, 1996) – will be fully evidenced.

An enhancement of the social work role?
The projects created an opportunity to examine the contribution of social workers to community care, and to observe at first hand the practice of social workers. Reference has already been made to the numerous organisational benefits accrued. However, the purpose of this section is to identify the distinctive contributions of social work to the successful multidisciplinary working which the projects have illustrated.

There were a number of ways in which social work played a distinctive role amongst the range of other services. One case from Project 3 exemplifies many of these. Mrs North was a single parent, in her forties, who was terminally ill with cancer. She was in receipt of home care, meals, attended by a district nurse daily, and had also received an occupational therapy assessment. A complicating factor was that she had a son with mild learning disabilities, who was in his early twenties; he seemed unable or unwilling to grasp the nature of her illness, causing his mother considerable anxiety. The social worker was initially involved in a review of her care needs, an assessment that was carried out with the close cooperation of the district nurse and GP. Mrs North was anxious that the outcome of the review would be an admission to nursing home care, which she was desperate to avoid. The social worker sought to enable her to maintain at home by intensifying the care package, which required continued close monitoring. In addition, work was identified to help her son come to grips with what was happening to his mother, and to start to prepare him both for her death and his life thereafter.

It was essential to have one person responsible for linking all other services together, with the capacity to respond swiftly to changing need. The social worker's location within the health centre made the liaison aspects of the role much more straightforward and facilitated a more coordinated and integrated approach. The way in which the social worker addressed the problem was responsive to Mrs North's wishes and concerns, and led to an outcome with which she was satisfied. The work that was initiated with her son demonstrated the ongoing need for social workers to use counselling skills, made more complex by his limited cognitive abilities. On several occasions, the social worker needed to apply professional judgements to the complicated set of circumstances with which she was confronted. This was not a case that could be resolved through simple adherence to procedural guidance, as it required the social worker to negotiate a shifting network of service provision, and balance the emotional needs of both Mrs North and her son.

Although cases of this level of complexity were not always encountered, and it is fair to observe that the project social workers dealt with their share of routine work, the example does indicate the professional significance of social work within the primary health care setting. We also reiterate the high levels of professional satisfaction reported by the project social workers, who appreciated the flexibility and relative autonomy they possessed in their day-to-day practice, and felt that their work had been both interesting and worthwhile. Such a perspective contrasts markedly with some of the more critical evaluations of the impact of community care on the professional role of social work (Lymbery, 1998b), and leads us to believe that this form of organisation may be professionally more fulfilling for social workers. In any case, as Simic (1997) reminds us, the significance of the development of PCGs to social work must be acknowledged, and can potentially be trans-formed into an opportunity for social work to re-establish a clear professional identity and direction (see also Lymbery, 1999).

Conclusion

As we have indicated throughout this discussion, there are fundamental benefits to be secured by locating social work within primary health care settings. We have argued that this would be a move in line with government thinking on the development of partnership between health and social care, that it enhances the level of professional satisfaction experienced by social workers, and that it provides an opportunity for excellent multidisciplinary practice. We have also pointed to some of the factors that may inhibit the development of this policy, which would represent a radical step for many SSDs. However, some departments – for example, Camden and Wiltshire – already base most or all of their community care services within primary health care settings. Therefore, we recommend that other SSDs should give this policy option their careful consideration.

The name of the service user referred to in this section has been anonymised.

References

Balloch, S (1998) 'New partnerships for social services' in Jones, H and MacGregor, S (eds) *Social Issues and Party Politics* London, Routledge

Beattie, A (1994) 'Healthy alliances or dangerous liaisons? The challenge of working together in health promotion' in Leathard, A (ed) *Going Inter-Professional: working together for health and welfare* London, Routledge

Bruce, N (1980) *Teamwork for Preventive Care* Chichester, John Wiley/Research Studies

Butrym, Z and Horder, J (1983) *Health, Doctors and Social Workers* London, Routledge and Kegan Paul

Bywaters, P (1986) 'Social work and the medical profession – arguments against unconditional collaboration' *British Journal of Social Work*, 16(6) pp 661–77

(CAIPE) Centre for the Advancement of Interprofessional Education (1996) *Sustaining Collaboration Between General Practitioners and Social Workers* London, CAIPE

Cairns Smith, D A (1989) 'Health centre social work – plugging the gap? A comparative study of client groups using a health centre and an area office' in Taylor, R and Ford, J (eds) *Social Work and Health Care* London, Jessica Kingsley

Challis, L and Pearson, J (1993) *Report on the Evaluation of Link Worker Pilots in Wiltshire* University of Bath, School of Social Sciences

Clare, A W and Corney, R H (1982) 'Social work and primary care: problems and possibilities' in Clare, A W and Corney, R H (eds.) *Social Work in Primary Health Care* London, Academic Press

Clark, H, Dyer, S and Horwood, J (1998) '*That Bit of Help': the high value of low level preventative services for older people* Bristol, Policy Press/Community Care

Collins, J (1965) *Social Casework in a General Medical Practice* London, Pitman Medical Publishing

Community Care (1999) 'Sparks fly over plans to take over failing departments', Community Care, 2–8 December, pp 10–11

Corney, R H (1980) 'Factors affecting the operation and success of social work attachment schemes to general practice' *Journal of the Royal College of General Practitioners* 30, pp 149-58

Corney, R H and Bowen, B A (1982) 'Referrals to social workers: a comparative study of a local authority intake team with a general practice attachment scheme' in Clare, A W and Corney, R H (eds) *Social Work in Primary Health Care* London, Academic Press

Corney, R H and Briscoe, M E (1977) 'Social workers and their clients: a comparison between primary health care and local authority settings' *Journal of the Royal College of General Practitioners* 27, pp 295–301

Craig, G and Manthorpe, J (1998) 'Small is beautiful?: local government reorganization and social services departments' *Policy and Politics* 26(2) pp 189–207

Cumella, S, le Mesurier, N and Tomlin, H (1996) *Social Work in Practice: An Evaluation of the Care Management Received by Elderly People from Social Workers Based in GP Practices in South Worcestershire* Birmingham, Martley

Dalley, G (1989) 'Professional ideology and organisational tribalism? The health service – social work divide', in Taylor, R and Ford, J (eds) *Social Work and Health Care* London, Jessica Kingsley

Dedman, G (1996) '1946 – 1973 reconstruction and integration: social work in the National Health Service', in Baraclough, J *et al.*, (eds), *100 Years of Health Related Social Work* Birmingham, Venture

DETR (Department of the Environment, Transport and the Regions) (1998) *Modernising Local Government: improving local services through best value* London, DETR

Dingwall, R (1982) 'Problems of Teamwork in Primary Care', in Clare, A W and Corney, R H (eds) *Social Work and Primary Health Care* London, Academic

DoH (Department of Health) (1989) *Caring for People: community care in the next decade and beyond* Cmnd 849, London, HMSO

DoH (Department of Health) (1990) *Community Care in the Next Decade and Beyond: policy guidance* London, HMSO

DoH (Department of Health) (1997a) *Social Services: achievement and challenge* Cmnd 3588, London, HMSO

DoH (Department of Health) (1997b) *The New NHS: Modern – dependable* Cmnd 3807, London, HMSO

DoH (Department of Health) (1998a) *Partnership in Action: a discussion document* London, Department of Health

DoH (Department of Health) (1998b) *Modernising Health and Social Services: national priorities guidance 1999/00 – 2001/02* London, Department of Health

DoH (Department of Health) (1998c) *Modernising Social Services* Cmnd. 4169, London, HMSO

DoH (Department of Health) (1999a) *The Relationship Between Health and Social Services* Cmnd. 4320, London, Stationery Office

DoH (Department of Health) (1999b) *Primary Care Groups: taking the next steps*: HSC 1999/246 LAC (99) 40, London, Department of Health

DoH (Department of Health) (1999c) *The Personal Social Services Performance Assessment Framework* London, Department of Health

DoH (Department of Health) (1999d) *Of Primary Importance: inspection of social services departments' links with primary health services – older people* London, Department of Health/Social Services Inspectorate

Everitt, A (1996) 'Developing critical evaluation' *Evaluation* 2(2) pp 173–88

Forman, J and Fairbairn, E (1968) *Social Casework in General Practice* Oxford, Oxford University Press

George, V and Wilding, P (1994) *Ideology and Social Welfare* Hemel Hempstead, Harvester Wheatsheaf

Goldberg, E M and Neill J E (1972) *Social Work and General Practice* London, George Allen and Unwin

Graham, H and Sher, M (1976) 'Social work and general medical practice: personal accounts of a three-year attachment' *British Journal of Social Work* 6 (2) pp 233–49

Gregson, B, Cartlidge, A and Bond, J (1991) *Interprofessional Collaboration in Primary Health Care Organizations: Occasional Paper 52* London, Royal College of General Practitioners

Hadley, R and Clough, R (1996) *Care in Chaos* London, Cassell

Hakim, C (1987) *Research Design: strategies and choices in the design of social research* London, Allen and Unwin

Hardy, B, Leedham, I and Wistow, G (1996) 'Care Manager Co-Location in GP Practices: Effects on Assessment and Care Management Arrangements for Older People' in Bland, R (ed) *Developing Services for Older People and their Families* London, Jessica Kingsley

Harris, J (1998) 'Scientific management, bureau-professionalism, new managerialism: The labour process of state social work' *British Journal of Social Work* 28 (6)pp 839–62

Higgins, R (1994) 'Working together: lessons for collaboration between health and social services' *Health and Social Care in the Community* 2, pp 269–77

Howe, D (1994) 'Modernity, postmodernity and social work' *British Journal of Social Work* 24 (5) pp 513–32

Hudson, B, Hardy, B, Henwood, M and Wistow, G (1997) 'Working across professional boundaries: primary health care and social care' *Public Money and Management* October – December, pp 25–30

Hudson, B (1999a) 'Primary health care and social care: working across professional boundaries: Part 1 – The changing context of inter-professional relationships' *Managing Community Care* 7 (1) pp 15–22

Hudson, B (1999b) 'Primary health care and social care: working across professional boundaries: Part 2 – Models of inter-professional collaboration' *Managing Community Care* 7 (2) pp 15–20

Hugman, R (1995) 'Contested territory and community services: Interprofessional boundaries in health and social care' in Soothill, K, Mackay, L and Webb, C (eds) *Interprofesional Relations in Health Care* London, Edward Arnold

Huntington, J (1981) *Social Work and General Medical Practice* London, George Allen and Unwin

Jefferys, M (1995) 'Primary health care', in Owens, P, Carrier, J and Horder, J (eds) *Interprofessional Issues in Community and Primary Health Care* Basingstoke, Macmillan

Langan, M (1993) 'The rise and fall of social work' in Clarke, J (ed) *A Crisis in Care* London, Sage/Open University

Langan, M and Clarke, J (1994) 'Managing in the mixed economy of care' in Clarke, J, Cochrane, A and McClaughlin, E (eds) *Managing Social Policy* London, Sage/Open University

Lewis, J and Glennerster, H (1996) *Implementing the New Community Care* Buckingham, Open University Press

Lymbery, M (1998a) 'Social Work in general practice: dilemmas and solutions' *Journal of Interprofessional Care* 12 (2) pp 199–208

Lymbery, M (1998b) 'Care management and professional autonomy: the impact of community care legislation on social work with older people' *British Journal of Social Work* 28 (6) pp 863–78

Lymbery, M (1999) 'Lessons from the past – learning for the future: social work in primary health care' *Practice* 11 (4) pp 5–14

Lymbery, M and Millward, A (1998) 'Community care in practice: social work in primary health care', paper presented to the 2nd International Conference on Social Work in Health and Mental Health, Melbourne, Australia, January 1998

Marshall, C and Rossman, G (1989) *Designing Qualitative Research* Newbury Park CA, Sage

McIntosh, J and Bennett-Emslie, G (1993) 'The health centre as a location for care management' *Health and Social Care in the Community* 1 (2) pp 91–7

Osborn, H (1996) 'One door – many mansions: 1974 – 1995', in Baraclough, J *et al.*, (eds.) *100 Years of Health Related Social Work* Birmingham, Venture

Otton Report (1974) *Report of the Working Party on Social Work Support for the Health Service* London, HMSO

Patton, M Q (1978) *Utilization-Focused Evaluation* Newbury Park CA: Sage

Patton, M Q (1980) *Qualitative Evaluation Methods* Newbury Park CA: Sage

Pithouse, A and Butler, I (1994) 'Social work attachment in a group practice' *Research, Policy and Planning* 12 (1) pp 16–20

Poxton, R (1999a) *Partnerships in Primary and Social Care* London, King's Fund

Poxton, R (ed) (1999b) *Working Across the Boundaries* London, King's Fund

Ratoff, L (1973) 'More social work for general practice?' *Journal of the Royal College of General Practitioners* 23, pp 736–42

Ratoff, L, Rose, A and Smith, C (1974) 'Social workers and general practitioners: some problems of working together' *Journal of the Royal College of General Practitioners* 24, pp 750–60

Rushton, A and Briscoe, M (1981) 'Social work as an aspect of primary health care: the social worker's view' *British Journal of Social Work* 11 (1) pp 61 – 76

Rushton, A and Davies, P (1984) *Social Work and Health Care* London, Heinemann

Russell Hodgson, C (1998) 'It's all good practice: linking primary care and social services in Greenwich' *Journal of Interprofessional Care* 12 (1) pp 89–93

Seebohm, F (1968) *Report of the Committee on Local Authority and Allied Personal Social Services* London, HMSO

Sheppard, M (1983) 'Referrals for general practitioners to a social services department' *Journal of the Royal College of General Practitioners* 33, pp 33–39

Simic, P (1997) 'Social work, primary care and organisational and professional change' *Research, Policy and Planning* 15 (1) pp 1–7

Sturges, P (1996) 'Care management practice: lessons from the USA' in Clark, C and Lapsley, L (eds) *Planning and Costing Care in the Community* London, Jessica Kingsley

Younghusband, E (1959) *Report of the Working Party on Social Workers in the Local Authority Health and Welfare Services* London, HMSO

Chapter 2
Locality and Hospital Based Social Work

Sarah Webb and Enid Levin

Introduction

The end of the twentieth century was a time of the most fundamental changes in local authority social services departments (SSDs) since their creation in 1971 and absorption of social workers employed by the health service in 1974. These developments were driven by the health and social care policy agendas of successive governments, went through several phases and are set to continue.

The first wave of change was triggered by The Children Act 1989 and the full implementation of The NHS and Community Care Act 1990 and related guidance in 1993. This legislation laid new duties on social services, shifted the balance and emphasis of the work of front-line staff, and accelerated the already existing trend from genericism to specialisation in work with specific service user groups.

Although structural transformation was not prescribed, SSDs reorganised as part of their implementation strategy. Despite differences in detail, the development of two broad divisions in each department was the common characteristic of the new arrangements, and work with children and families is now managed and undertaken separately from work with other user groups.

Across SSDs a variety of arrangements emerged in the community care branch of the operation but all continued to locate some practitioners in hospitals (Challis *et al.*, 1998; DoH, 1998). Discrete area teams for learning disabilities are common, as are community mental health teams run jointly with health. In the case of older people and disabled people, some SSDs opt for teams which cover both groups, others for separate teams for each group and yet others further subdivide their work with older people into those with and without mental health problems. These structural realignments created new interfaces within SSDs at a time when working across the borders with health and other agencies assumed increasing importance.

The new care management arrangements had just bedded down and become understood by service users and by professionals in other agencies when the change of government precipitated a second wave of new developments. The policy thrust towards promoting public health and modernising both health and local government services, and the mechanisms to achieve improvements and regulate services have been set out in a steady stream of White and Green Papers, guidance, circulars and legislation. As Hunter (1998) has pointed out, the watchwords of policy are clear – partnerships, alliances, collaboration, integrated care, and tackling inequalities.

The rapidly moving agenda is underpinned by the new duty of partnership between health and local government and by new opportunities for pooled budgets. Thus health authorities have the lead role for primary care groups/trusts, health improvement programmes, health action zones and healthy living centres but these developments have to be carried out in partnerships with local authorities.

Whilst the changes, especially greater integration between social and health care, work their way through the systems, both continuities and discontinuities between the old and new ways of working can be identified. Two continuities are relevant to the focus of this chapter on front-line social work practice with older people. These are the robustness of the team model of organisation in social services and the theme of working closely with health service practitioners.

First, enduring features of all SSDs are the area and hospital based teams through which front-line services are largely delivered. In their Scottish study, Tibbitt and Martin (1991) drew attention to this common characteristic of departments, whatever the geographical scope, organisational structure and range of needs to be met. They commented also on the variety of models on which area teams were organised and on the lack of research into the consequences of different forms of organisation for the outcomes that can be achieved for clients. In Scotland, England and Wales, the area team arrangement still predominates in mainstream services. It is the base of a flurry of activity to facilitate closer working with health. This includes aligning practitioners with primary care groups, moving the teams into health centres, nominating workers to link with specific GPs and nurses, and creating joint health and social care teams, albeit more rapidly for some user groups, such as mental health, than for others (SSI, 1998a).

The second enduring feature of social work in SSDs is collaboration with the health service. As the Introduction observes, in practice, health and welfare agencies have a long tradition of working together. This stretches back to the appointment of Mary Stewart as the social worker for the Royal Free Hospital in London in 1895 and forward throughout the lifetime of the welfare state.

Although social work in hospitals is an underresearched area, about one-fifth of social workers are based there. Reviews of research (Sinclair *et al.*, 1990) show that health professionals are a major source of referrals to social services area teams. As many policy analysts have pointed out (Parsloe, 1981; Sheppard, 1992; Wistow, 1994; Challis, 1998; Hunter, 1998), the exhortations to collaborate, cooperate and coordinate abound. They run through the official documents of the 1970s which introduced new mechanisms for consultation at the strategic and planning levels and for jointly financed initiatives, and also through the guidance on both children's and community care services in the early 1990s.

Nonetheless, the emphasis on partnership working at all levels in the operation of health and social services seems stronger than ever before, and the question is no longer whether services should work together but how they will work together (Lewis, 1998). The underlying assumptions of the policy are that closer working will lead to better quality and higher standards of service, and that the greater the degree of collaboration, the better the outcomes for patients and service users. In several respects, policy and practice developments are ahead of research, in that some SSDs have begun to align services with primary care groups.

The hypothesis that some models of collaboration lead to better outcomes than others has until recently been largely untried and untested in systematic studies. However, a series of projects have sought the practitioners' views of the effects of schemes such as social work attachment or alignment with general practice, and identified the factors that promote and hinder collaboration (Standing Medical and Nursing & Midwifery Advisory Committees, 1996; Vanclay, 1996). They report consistently that one benefit of closer working is a clearer understanding among doctors, social workers and nurses of each others' roles, responsibilities, agency function, pressure of work and of the ways that they spend their time. Indeed, Chapter 1 of this book provides a recent example of the benefits of such a realignment.

As health and social services embark on a new set of changes, it is important to take stock and consider the current role of social work. What do social workers do? What skills and knowledge do they need? How do they spend their time at work? With whom do they have contact during their working day? How do the jobs of social workers based in a health setting differ from the jobs of those based in the community? This chapter provides baseline information on what social workers were doing three years after the implementation of community care. It uses data from one of the first studies following the community care changes to document the work of social work staff in both hospital and locality based teams.

First, we shall describe the study and the SSDs who were our partners in the research. Then we shall outline some of the findings from the study, focusing in particular on a comparison of social workers based in area teams with those working in hospital teams. We shall look at their views on the impact of the new arrangements on their jobs. We shall outline the tasks that they undertook, look at the way that they spent their time on their last day at work, and describe their last assessment of need. Finally, we shall consider the implications of these findings for health-related social work and the move towards integrated care.

The National Institute for Social Work (NISW) Social Work and Community Care Study

Since April 1993 a new body of research on the work of social services in the context of the community care changes has emerged. This includes work on the mapping of care management arrangements (Challis *et al.*, 1998) and their implementation in England (Lewis and Glennerster, 1996), and research focusing on the new arrangements in Scotland (Petch *et al.*, 1996) and Wales (McGrath *et al.*, 1996). The NISW Social Work and Community Care study was part of a programme of research on community care commissioned by the Department of Health. A second complementary study focused on community care for older people with dementia (Moriarty and Webb, 2000). The Social Work and Community Care study was designed to document the roles and tasks of social workers under the new arrangements for community care. The study provides a quantitative benchmark in terms of the activities and use of time by social services staff three years after implementation of these arrangements and also gives an account of their views and experiences.

We undertook the research in three SSDs: a metropolitan district in the Midlands, an inner London borough and a large county in the south-east of England. The size and demographic characteristics of the populations served by these three SSDs varied, and there were differences in social services per capita expenditure and provision to the population aged 75 and over (Government Statistical Service, 1996). One common feature was the separation of services to children and families from those to adults. Each of the three areas had locality and hospital based teams providing services for adults and older people, but there were differences in terms of team size and composition and in arrangements for screening, initial assessment and care planning, and monitoring and review. The London borough was the only area with separate assessment and care management teams for older people.

The study included 629 staff based in a total of 52 locality and hospital teams for older people and disabled adults. We identified five types of job: team manager (n=73), social worker (n=368), social work assistant (n=128), information and advice worker (n=35) and nurse care manager (n=25). Overall, 25 per cent of the staff (n=156) worked in the 11 hospital based teams. The proportion of staff in hospitals varied from 30 per cent of staff in the metropolitan district to 23 per cent in the London borough, and 17 per cent in the county.

We compiled a list of current staff with the team leaders and sent each person a numbered questionnaire, personal letter and Freepost envelope addressed to the researchers. The questionnaire comprised 37 items. These included questions on: the respondents' personal characteristics; the content of their current job; their experiences of community care; the allocation of their time on the last day at work and, for those who carried out assessments, a series of questions covering the last assessment undertaken.

Overall, the response rate was 48 per cent. Thirty per cent of the questionnaires were returned after the first letter and a further 18 per cent were returned after one reminder. The response rate varied by area: 41 per cent of workers returned a questionnaire in the metropolitan district, 49 per cent in the London borough and 61 per cent in the county. The metropolitan district was completing a reorganisation, an upheaval that may have affected the response rate. Importantly, however, the response rate did not vary with job type or team location, and questionnaires were returned from all the teams approached. Thus we were able to compare the characteristics and responses of staff and to be reasonably confident that our sample was representative of the study population, namely front-line staff in the three SSDs. The response rate is similar to those reported in other surveys conducted since 1993 (McGrath *et al.*, 1996; Petch *et al.*, 1996). It should be considered in the context of an increase in paperwork reported by many social care practitioners, including those who participated in our study, and it has implications for other research focusing on front-line staff.

A total of 159 respondents whom we classified as social workers returned questionnaires. The vast majority (91 per cent) of this group reported their job title as social worker, senior social worker or senior practitioner, and the remainder were designated as care managers and worked in the discrete care management teams in the London borough. This is in line with work that mapped care management arrangements in 79 English authorities and found that London boroughs were more likely to use the term 'care managers' than other types of local authority (Challis *et al.*, 1998). As most of those undertaking assessment and care management comprised staff whom we classified as social workers, including the care managers, we will focus on this group of staff in our comparison of hospital based and locality based social work.

The social workers in the study
Of the 159 social workers returning questionnaires, 108 worked in locality teams and 51 were based in hospital social work teams. The characteristics of

the social workers in our sample were similar to those reported in other surveys of front-line social services staff (Balloch, McLean and Fisher, 1999; LGMB, 1997; Smyth, 1996). The majority (72 per cent) were women. The mean age of the social workers was 41, and 71 per cent were aged between 30 and 49. Eighty-two per cent of the social workers categorised themselves as white, 11 per cent as black and 4 per cent as Asian. There were no differences by age, gender or ethnic group between social workers in locality and hospital based teams but there were some differences by age and ethnic group between the study areas. Those working in the London borough were a younger group, probably reflecting greater stability in the workforce in the other two areas. None of the social workers in the county categorised themselves as black or Asian, compared with 17 per cent of the social workers in the metropolitan district, and 31 per cent in the London borough. These differences broadly reflected the ethnic composition of the populations served by the three SSDs (Government Statistical Service, 1996). Excluding the 11 social workers who held job-share posts, 16 per cent worked part-time (defined as less than 30 hours per week). The proportion of part-time social workers did not vary by team location but more women worked part-time than men.

A social work qualification was held by 93 per cent of the social workers. Fifty-eight per cent had attained a Certificate of Qualification in Social Work (CQSW), 31 per cent held a Diploma in Social Work (DipSW) and 12 per cent had a Certificate in Social Services (CSS). Other qualifications included postgraduate social work awards and social work qualifications from abroad. Not surprisingly, Smyth's survey (1996) carried out three years earlier, found a higher proportion of staff with a CQSW and fewer with a DipSW. Compared with the metropolitan district and the county, a slightly higher proportion of social workers in the London borough held a DipSW, reflecting the younger staff group in this area. We found no other differences in type of social work qualification by study area, team location or gender.

Social workers' views on the impact of the community care changes
Across all three SSDs we found strong support for the concept of community care in the sense of enabling people to live at home for as long as possible if this was what they wanted.

Regardless of their place of work, social workers were most likely to identify the new arrangements for assessment and care management as having the greatest impact on their jobs. These were said to have made the work more manageable and at the same time more managed. On the one hand, there was more clarity in working with service users, especially over eligibility criteria, and more flexibility in planning packages of care. On the other hand, the new arrangements had also led to the work being more managed, resulting in practice becoming more defensive. One social worker remarked: 'The emphasis has moved from good practice to accountable practice – these are not necessarily the same thing.'

Other social workers referred to the lessening of professional control or autonomy, to a greater superficiality in their work and to working in a reactive rather than a proactive way. Many staff felt that the new focus on assessment and care management had encroached upon the time for other activities. As one social worker explained: 'Assessment has come to be seen as a service in itself and there is less time to concentrate on people in complex situations.'

As we shall show, this was a recurrent theme.

The separation of the purchasing and providing functions and the increasing emphasis on the mixed economy of care were also mentioned frequently by social workers. These developments had expanded the scope of their work in terms of care planning and service coordination. New tasks included negotiating with the independent sector, costing care packages, writing contracts and monitoring service quality. The advantages of working with more than one service sector stemmed from being able to plan and set up packages more effectively, but there were drawbacks. Some social workers expressed concerns over the time-consuming nature of purchasing services from private agencies and of monitoring and reviewing those services. There were fewer opportunities for face-to-face contact with staff from independent agencies than there were with in-house providers. This had implications for the responsiveness of services and for feedback and monitoring.

One small interview study found that social workers based in hospitals felt particularly excluded from the process of change in the run-up to community care (La Valle and Lyons, 1996), even though, arguably, they encountered more change than their colleagues in area based teams. As well as preparing for the implementation of the new arrangements for assessment and care management, hospital social workers faced the introduction of jointly agreed hospital discharge procedures. One perceived change in their role, mourned by some hospital social workers in the NISW study, was the new emphasis on planning for discharge at the expense of counselling people with serious health problems and their families. This issue has also been reported in two other studies focusing on hospital social workers since April 1993 (Davies and Connolly, 1995; Rachman, 1995), and is further discussed in Chapter 3.

Some hospital social workers felt that other professionals, particularly nurses, were encroaching on their role by undertaking more counselling. Compared to locality based staff, hospital social workers reported a faster turnover of work. There were reports, too, of pressure from medical and nursing staff to discharge patients quickly in each of the three study areas. One social worker commented: '[We] can only work on a fairly superficial level as greater numbers pass through hospital more quickly.'

As the community care changes were being implemented, concurrent changes in the NHS meant that the boundaries between the acute and community health sectors were being redrawn, and raised questions about the potential for increased collaboration (Wistow, 1994). The separation of the purchasing and providing functions in SSDs and in the NHS increased the number of inter-faces to be managed within and between the two agencies (Higgins, Oldham and Hunter, 1994). Caldock (1994, p.140) warned that policies stating that professionals should work together are not sufficient to effect change in the context of 'a contradictory and conflicting reality in which the dynamics and pressures present may be acting tangentially to the spirit of the reforms'.

The assignment of the lead role for care management to social services had opened up the way for a more equal partnership with health professionals, but in practice social workers' experiences varied. Some social workers reported that the changes had led to improvements in communication and information-sharing, and more opportunities for multidisciplinary work. For others, little seemed to have changed. Reported problems included an increase in inappropriate referrals as hospital staff failed to make allowance for new eligibility criteria. One hospital social worker explained: 'It is somewhat obvious that we work on two different wavelengths with little understanding of what each other is about.' In contrast, another social worker wrote: 'I am fortunate in working with a medical team that are sympathetic to people's needs.'

One change appreciated by both hospital and locality based social workers was an improvement in links and communication between social services staff in hospitals and the community. The practice of transferring cases back to area teams a few weeks after hospital discharge had increased the opportunities for liaison between hospital and locality based staff.

Although we found a range of views on which of the community care changes had had the most impact on the jobs of social workers, there was overall agreement on the main difference that implementation of the community care legislation had made to their day-to-day work. Irrespective of study area or place of work, social workers were likely to identify an increase in paperwork, resulting in a greater proportion of time being spent at their desks and less time with service users, as the main difference in their work compared to before 1993. One locality based social worker perceptively wrote:

The amount of administration and paperwork has increased dramati-cally at the same time as a reduction in admin. support. Probably only 20 per cent of my time is spent in customer contact and even that amount leads to a backlog of admin. jobs.

Another area social worker commented: 'I trained to work with people, not fill out endless forms.'

Nobody was of the opinion that all of the paperwork was unnecessary, as filling in forms and keeping records had always been part of the social workers' tasks. Rather it was the marked increase in the volume of paperwork associated with each part of the care management process that was an issue. In some cases, workers were required to write the same information out up to ten times on ten different forms when completing an assessment and arranging services for one individual. Apart from keeping records up to date, other paperwork to be completed included assessment forms, financial assessment forms, care plans, hospital discharge plans, referral forms for other agencies, service contracts, residential care placement agreements, spot contracts, review forms, case closure forms, workload monitoring forms and statistical returns. As in the study reported in Chapter 3, social workers referred to the mountain of paperwork and to the paper chase. They described themselves as submerged, drowning, bogged down and overwhelmed by large amounts of paperwork, much of it repetitive. One social worker with no access to secretarial or clerical help on site wrote:

There are days when it feels as if the service users could tiptoe quietly away and no-one would notice. The paper chain of assessment, criteria matching, care planning and review would go on with its own momentum.

The tasks of the social workers
Prior to implementation, one key debate centred on which occupational groups were best suited to carry out care management. Although SSDs were the lead agency, *Caring for People* had proposed that other professional groups such as occupational therapists and community nurses would make suitable care managers (DoH, 1989).

Sheppard (1995) and Payne (1995) both made strong cases for the particular relevance of the social work approach and orientation to the practice of care management. However, there were concerns about the implications of adopting a care management role for social work practice. Challis (1994) warned that too rigid an interpretation of the roles of purchaser and provider could lead to an administrative form of care management where care managers principally purchase services, rather than a clinical model which would include support and counselling as part of the care manager's job. Fisher (1991) questioned whether the assessor should undertake ongoing work such as counselling. He argued that if direct work using social work skills was part of care manage-ment, it should be focused on the achievement of specific goals rather than on deriving therapeutic benefit from the relationship. In Scotland, Petch and colleagues (1996) found that in the two 'task model' regions where care management was undertaken alongside other professional tasks practitioners were more likely to be providing counselling than were practitioners operating as care managers in two 'role model' regions. By contrast, the Welsh survey of front-line staff with an assessment and/or care management role found little difference between care managers and social workers in the proportions reporting that they undertook direct work (McGrath *et al.*, 1996).

In the NISW study, the social workers' written responses to open questions showed that they considered that their jobs had changed substantially as a con-sequence of the new arrangements for community care. We also asked them to complete a checklist comprising 20 tasks. These were: taking referrals, making referrals, advice and information, assessment of needs, financial assessment, devising care plans, purchasing services, coordinating services, monitoring, review, outreach, group work, counselling, liaison work, managing staff, super-vising practice, managing a budget, allocating referrals, training staff and policy work. This list includes the core assessment and care management tasks set out in practice guidance (SSI/SWSG, 1991), as well as other activities previously associated with casework such as counselling, outreach and group work.

As expected, we found that the vast majority of social workers were under-taking the core care management tasks of assessment (99 per cent), devising care plans (99 per cent), coordinating services (96 per cent), monitoring (97 per cent) and review (97 per cent). Although 89 per cent of social workers reported that they were purchasing services, only 6 per cent were managing a budget. At the time of the study, budgets had not been devolved to practition-ers in the three SSDs and were almost always held at team manager level. This arrangement reflected the departments' policies that assessments of need should be made independently from budgetary responsibilities. Other work suggests that this is also a common arrangement elsewhere (Challis *et al.*, 1998; Lewis and Glennerster, 1996; McGrath *et al.*, 1996; SSI, 1998a).

All the social workers indicated that providing information and advice was part of their job, including those who worked alongside information and advice staff in locality teams in two SSDs. The vast majority reported that they took referrals (98 per cent).

Financial assessments were being carried out by 94 per cent of the social workers. Their subsequent comments suggested that some of them did not feel that this should be part of their job. One social worker wrote: 'I didn't enter the profession to look at how much money people have to contribute to their care.' And another explained: 'Financial assessments . . . take up a lot of time and could in fact be done by a clerk. Clients are sometimes resentful at having to pay for services and this can make our relationship strained.'

On the other hand, 80 per cent of the social workers felt that they were unable to do things which should be part of their job, and many of these identified counselling as one of the main roles which had been lost.

The role of social workers as counsellors and providers of emotional support has long been a matter of debate. In their Seatown study, Goldberg and Warburton (1979) showed that the help provided to the great majority of older people by social workers was concerned with arranging direct practical assistance such as home care, meals services, day care and residential care. As we noted earlier, there is some more recent evidence that social work practitioners undertaking care management alongside other professional tasks were more likely to be providing counselling than those operating as care managers (Petch *et al.*, 1996).

In our study, only one of the SSDs had separate assessment and care management teams but the perception that their opportunities for counselling or casework were reduced was mentioned by some social workers in each of the three areas. Although a few social workers directly related this to changes in their role, many more explained that the pressure of work due to the volume of referrals, increased caseloads or paperwork meant that there was simply less or no time at all to carry out therapeutic work with service users. This was seen by the social workers as one deleterious consequence of the changes. One hospital social worker wrote: 'Social work has changed . . . but emotions don't change. People still feel angry, distressed, bemused, bewildered at what is happening to them.'

The comments may be borne out by the finding that 54 per cent of social workers indicated that they were counselling service users or their families as part of their job. Far fewer were undertaking outreach work (13 per cent) or group work (13 per cent). Before 1993 these tasks were key components of the community social work role. Indeed, Payne (1995) suggested that they were crucial if the objectives of community care policy were to be achieved.

In this study, the findings that the proportions of social workers undertaking counselling, group work and outreach work were much smaller than the proportions undertaking assessment and care management tasks suggests that the balance of their jobs may have changed. The more traditional tasks associated with casework may have been overtaken by those which are involved in assessment, providing practical assistance, and information and advice to the individual. This shift in emphasis has been identified in other studies in England (Davies and Connolly, 1995; Rachman, 1995; Lewis and Glennerster, 1996; Irving and Gertig, 1998). However, in a survey in Wales, 91 per cent of front-line staff indicated that they counselled users or families (McGrath *et al.*, 1996).

Social workers based in locality teams and in hospital teams were equally likely to report that they undertook each of the tasks, suggesting that the main activities of the practitioners in the two settings are broadly similar. Other findings from this study show important differences between the work of the two groups. One key contrast is the mean number of cases held by workers in the two settings. A comparison of the caseloads of full-time social workers showed that those in locality based teams held a mean of 41 cases compared to a mean of 27 cases for those based in hospital teams. The difference reflects the practice in all three SSDs of transferring cases back to staff in area teams a few weeks after discharge from hospital. It is consistent with the practitioners' reports of a much faster turnover of cases in the hospital setting, resulting in fewer opportunities to undertake long-term work.

The skills and knowledge that social workers require
The NISW workforce studies found that 70 per cent of social work staff had qualified before 1989 (Balloch *et al.*, 1999). The qualifications held by the social workers in this study and their comments on the questionnaires indicated that the majority had started to practise before the changes to community care.

Some acknowledged that the changes had given them the opportunity to acquire new skills and knowledge, particularly in relation to the new tasks associated with purchasing. The skills that they listed included financial skills, especially budget management, and a growing need to acquire computing skills to be able to make best use of newly introduced computer based recording and information systems.

Although a few social workers commented that they felt deskilled or that their professional social work skills had been devalued as a result of the changes, many more emphasised their continuing relevance. One social worker based in an area team described the challenge of ensuring 'that social work skills are not being diluted by other pressures.'

From a wide range of skills identified by the social workers, communication and listening were mentioned most frequently. Others commenting on the applicability of social work practice to care management have drawn similar conclusions about the continuing importance and applicability of interpersonal skills (Smale and Tuson, 1993; Payne, 1995; Sheppard, 1995). One project which invited service users' and carers' organisations to define quality in social work practice showed that communication and listening skills are highly valued by users and carers (Harding and Beresford, 1996).

It was interesting that social workers in both locality and hospital teams mentioned the importance of skills in working with health professionals. These encompassed communication skills, the competence to liaise and negotiate with other professionals and, for hospital based staff, the ability to work within a multidisciplinary team. Hospital social workers in particular identified educating their health colleagues about the role and values of social work as an important part of their job.

The social workers commented that many types of knowledge were required to carry out their jobs. As well as an understanding of the relevant legislation, national policy guidance and local policies and procedures, they needed to be able to access up-to-date information on social care services in the statutory and independent sectors, community health services, welfare rights and local budgets.

One type of knowledge mentioned more often but not exclusively by hospital based social workers was an understanding of medical terminology and health problems. The study discussed in Chapter 3 which included direct observation of assessors working on specific cases, found that the information supplied by hospital doctors and GPs about patients' medical conditions was often not adequate for the assessment (Manthorpe, *et al.*, 1996). In such cases, the assessor sought the relevant details from another informant, such as a nurse.

Use of time
The jobs of social workers in locality and hospital teams appeared to be broadly similar in terms of whether or not specific tasks comprised part of their remit and also in terms of the skills and knowledge required for their work. Therefore, a key question is whether there were any differences in the way that they spent their time.

Previous research has used time diaries completed over a period of one or two weeks or longer (Carver and Edwards, 1972; Law, 1982; Connor and Tibbitt, 1988). Such an approach was not feasible in our study and so we developed a simple measure for inclusion in the self-completion questionnaire.

Respondents were asked to write in the number of minutes that they had spent on each of six broad activities on their previous day at work. The activities were: face-to-face contact with service users; face-to-face contact with professionals; telephone work; computer work; other administrative work, including paperwork; and travel. A category of 'other' was also included, and respondents were asked to specify how any time entered under this heading had been used.

The time allocation exercise was completed by 94 per cent of social workers. We analysed the data in two main ways. First, we examined the proportion of time spent on the different activities by all respondents on their previous day at work. Second, we calculated the mean amount of time spent on each activity by full-time staff.

Fig. 2.1 Proportion of social workers' time spent on activities on the previous day at work, by team location

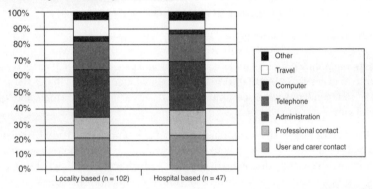

We have already shown how the social workers themselves considered that the changes had led to a reduction in the amount of time they were able to spend with users and their families. To what extent were their perceptions supported by the quantitative data on time use?

Figure 2.1 shows the proportion of time spent on the seven types of activities by hospital and locality based social workers on their previous day at work. Overall, the way in which they divided their time between these broad categories was very similar. Full-time staff spent an average of eight hours at work, excluding breaks. Almost all the social workers reported face-to-face contact with service users or carers on their previous day at work. Regardless of their place of work, one-fifth of time was spent in this way. This means that those working full-time spent an average of just over one and a half hours in face-to-face contact with users or carers on their previous day at work.

It is interesting that care managers were reported to spend one-fifth of their time in contact with service users in one area studied by Lewis and Glennerster (1996) and that this is also the figure estimated by the hospital social workers in Rachman's study (1995). Although these data have been interpreted as signifying a reduction in time spent with clients, to what extent is this borne out by research carried out before April 1993? The evidence is equivocal. Comparisons between studies of time use are not straightforward because of differences in the study samples, design, and the ways in which categories of activity have been defined.

One of the earliest studies carried out in 18 pre-Seebohm health and welfare departments in 1969 found that there were close similarities between health and welfare services in 'the broad apportioning of time' (Carver and Edwards, 1972). Overall 30 per cent of time worked was accounted for by 'case contact' time, a category that included 'discussion with clients' (19 per cent of time), discussion with others concerned (6 per cent), 'telephone interviews' (4 per cent) and travel with clients (2 per cent). A later study of hospital social work in one English SSD in 1976 found that 'casework activities' took up 45 per cent of time but that 'face-to-face discussion with clients and relatives' accounted for just 15 per cent (Law, 1982). However, another study concentrating on hospital social work in Scotland reported that social workers spent 33 per cent of their time in 'direct work with clients' (Connor and Tibbitt, 1988). All three studies found differences in the way time was spent by client group or specialty.

Whatever measure is used, it appears that face-to-face contact with clients has never accounted for more than about a third of total time spent at work. What may have changed substantially is *how* time is spent during meetings with clients, so that with the emphasis on completing the assessment process there is less time to undertake other activities such as providing emotional support.

Communicating with other professionals has always formed an important part of the social worker's job. In this study 87 per cent of the social workers reported that they spent some time on their previous day at work in face-to-face contact with other professionals. Eighteen out of the nineteen social workers who reported no face-to-face contact worked in an area team.

The hospital based social workers spent a greater part of their day in face-to-face contact with other professionals (on average, just under an hour and a half) compared to their locality based colleagues (just over an hour). The NISW study of community care for older people with dementia found that assessors based in hospital were more likely to report that they had carried out joint assessments (Moriarty and Webb, 2000). These findings are not surprising because hospital based staff have much greater opportunity for both formal and informal meetings with health professionals during their working day.

Figure 2.1 clearly shows that both locality based and hospital based social workers spent, on average, just under a third of their day on administrative tasks. Only one social worker reported that she had not spent any time on administrative tasks on her previous day at work. Ten per cent of social workers reported spending half their working time or longer on this activity. Although the Scottish study of hospital social work found that just 14 per cent of time was spent on 'reading background notes or writing reports' (Connor and Tibbitt, 1988), it is striking that the two earlier studies both reported very similar figures for time spent on 'desk jobs' (27 per cent) and 'administration' (30 per cent) (Carver and Edwards, 1972; Law, 1982). This shows that routine administrative tasks have always formed a substantial part of the social worker's job, but raises the important issue of whether these activities are the most appropriate use of social work time, as recognised in a recent report by the Social Services Inspectorate (SSI, 1998a).

Figure 2.1 also shows the importance of the telephone as a means of communication. Eighty-five per cent of the social workers reported spending 10 per cent or more of their time making or receiving telephone calls. In contrast, only 8 per cent of the social workers spent 10 per cent or more of their time using a computer. Fifty eight per cent had not used a computer at all on their previous day at work but the proportion of computer users varied by area. In the London borough which made the greatest use of information technology on the front line, 76 per cent of the social workers had spent time using a computer, compared with 42 per cent and 32 per cent in the metropolitan district and county respectively. Overall, using the computer accounted for just 3 per cent of the social workers' time.

As the NHS and social services make increasing use of computer systems to manage information at strategic and operational levels, social workers are likely to be spending a greater proportion of their time on this activity in the future. Perhaps it was their recognition of this development that made it one of the five most frequently mentioned areas in which they would have liked to receive more training.

Not surprisingly, the hospital based social workers spent less time on travel connected with their work. At ten minutes, this difference was smaller than expected and may be influenced both by an increase in home visiting by hospital social workers and by the large geographical areas covered by the hospital social work teams in the county. Thirty-four per cent of the social workers indicated that they had spent time on activities which fell outside the six main headings, including time spent attending interviews, training courses, team meetings and supervision.

In addition to completing the exercise on the use of time, the social workers were asked to indicate with whom they had contact on their previous day at work. Table 2.1 confirms that social workers in both locality and hospital settings deal with a diverse range of people on a day-to-day basis. Table 2.1 also shows that although the overall pattern of time use between locality based and hospital based social workers was similar, the detail did vary in terms of the type of face-to-face and telephone contacts on their previous day at work.

Table 2.1 Face-to-face and telephone contacts for social workers on the previous day at work, by team location

	All % ticked 'yes'	Locality based team % ticked 'yes'	Hospital based team % ticked 'yes'	
Face-to-face contact				
Service users or carers	90	86	98	*
Community health staff	18	19	16	
Hospital health staff	46	23	94	***
Senior managers in SSD	37	44	22	**
Independent sector	20	23	12	
Benefits Agency	3	4	0	
Telephone contact				
Service users or carers	82	83	78	
Community health staff	51	59	34	
Hospital health staff	53	52	56	
Senior managers in SSD	9	9	8	
Independent sector	63	67	54	
Benefits Agency	47	45	50	
Total n	*150*	*108*	*50*	

Key   * p>0.05, ** p>0.01, *** p>0.001

Whereas all the hospital social workers had seen at least one service user or carer, 14 per cent of locality based staff had not seen a user or carer on their previous day at work. This difference may be explained by the physical proximity of hospital social workers to their clients, most of whom are referred during a hospital stay. Discussion with practitioners suggested that the locality based workers were likely to visit greater numbers of service users and carers at home, a difference supported by the finding that they spent more of their time at work on travel.

Ninety per cent of the social workers had either face-to-face or telephone contact with at least one health professional. Not surprisingly, almost all the hospital based social workers had seen at least one hospital health profession-al on their last day at work and they were much more likely to have done so than locality based workers. Social workers in locality based teams were no more likely to have seen community based health staff but were more likely to have spoken to a health professional based in the community than their counterparts in the hospital teams.

Contacts with the independent sector were usually by telephone, a finding which is consistent with the social workers' comments on lack of face-to-face contact with providers from this sector. It was striking that almost half of the social workers had been in telephone contact with the Benefits Agency, confirming that service users and their families often require advice and information on claiming benefits and other financial matters. This was another area in which the social workers mentioned they would have liked further training.

Assessing need
As well as collecting information on the social workers' activities on their previous day at work, we asked them about the last assessment of need that they had undertaken. As many as 155 of the 159 social workers in our sample answered questions about the referral, the involvement of others in the assessment process, and the services provided following the assessment.

Referrals were most likely to have been made by hospital based health staff (46 per cent), the service user's family or friends (29 per cent), or community health professionals (22 per cent). These data are similar to referral patterns prior to the community care changes (Sinclair, *et al.*, 1990), and to those found in other recent research (Manthorpe *et al.*, 1996; Petch *et al.*, 1996). Ten per cent of referrals originated from other sources. These included wardens of sheltered accommoda-tion, voluntary organisations and day care or home care service providers.

As expected, there was variation in referral source by the type of team in which the social worker was based. Referrals to locality based teams were more likely to come from relatives or friends, or from community health services, than were those to hospital teams.

The great majority (89 per cent) of people assessed by the hospital social workers had been referred by hospital health professionals. Hospital referrals were most likely to be defined in broad general terms as requests for hospital discharge and less likely to relate specifically to the service user or carer. Social workers in the locality teams were more likely to have undertaken their last assessment of need with a person who had been referred for reasons relating to his or her carer. Often these referrals suggested situations that were on the point of breakdown or had been precipitated by some kind of crisis. One-quarter of the referrals were made for reasons related to the service user. These included those based on concerns about the service user's safety or neglect, and requests for more unspecified support.

The assessment rarely involved only the assessor and service user. Ninety-six per cent involved at least one other person and 59 per cent involved two or more others. In three-quarters of cases, a carer or family member was also present or consulted by the social worker. Community health staff, usually the district nurse or GP, were involved in just under half of assessments carried out by staff based in the community and in one in five of hospital based assessments. Conversely, hospital health staff were involved in three-quarters of hospital based assessments but in only one in six of those carried out by social workers based in the locality teams. Again, this pattern is consistent with the data reported above on the social workers' use of time and with data reported elsewhere (Manthorpe *et al.*, 1996; Moriarty and Webb, 2000; Petch *et al.*, 1996; SSI, 1998b).

Almost all the assessments undertaken by the social workers resulted in some kind of change in services. Only 11 assessments had not resulted in any service provision and in 6 of these no firm decisions regarding care packages had been reached. The majority of assessments (80 per cent) made by both the locality and the hospital based social workers resulted in a package of care at home. Eight per cent of assessments were followed by the service user's admission to permanent care.

Forty-seven per cent of the last assessments made by the social workers resulted in care packages using more than one type of sector. Inhouse services were more likely to be used for supporting people at home than for making long-term placements in residential care. However, half of the packages provided to people at home incorporated at least one service purchased from the independent sector. The pattern was reversed for long-term care placements of which four out of five were made in the independent sector. We found no differences in the use of inhouse, independent or voluntary sector services between social workers based in hospitals and their community based counterparts.

Thirty-nine per cent of social workers indicated that they were unable to provide at least one type of support, ranging from specific services such as bathing to limits on the amount of a service such as home care. It is not surprising that this proportion did not vary by work setting as all the assessors working within an SSD were subject to the same constraints in terms of financial ceilings on care package costs, budget sizes and available services.

Compared to the community based social workers, those working in hospitals were less likely to have offered support which had not been taken up by the service user or carer. One study which interviewed older people living in the community about their needs and access to services found that independence was given as a positive reason for managing without services (MacDonald, 1999). It may be the case that social services' clients in hospital are more likely to accept an offer of services as a means of returning home than people living in the community who may be concerned that accepting such an offer will encroach upon their independence.

Discussion
In this chapter we have presented findings from the NISW Social Work and Community Care study, focusing on the tasks and activities undertaken by hospital based and locality based social workers. Several key findings have important implications for health-related social work with disabled adults and older people.

The study provided information on the characteristics of staff based in hospital and area teams for disabled adults and older people. There were no differences in age, gender, ethnic group or professional qualification between social workers based in hospital and those based in locality teams. In line with other work (Balloch *et al.*, 1999; LGMB, 1997; Smyth, 1996), the social workers were predominantly women aged between 30 and 49 who worked full-time. An important finding is that the majority of staff undertaking assessment and care management tasks were qualified social workers. This is one consequence of structural reorganisation in response to The Children Act 1989 and The NHS and Community Care Act 1990. It means that older people in touch with social services are now more likely to have access to a qualified social worker, and suggests that the status of older people as service users within SSDs has risen (Manthorpe *et al.*, 1996).

The social workers themselves were committed to the concept of community care in terms of enabling people to live at home. Despite the changes that the new arrangements had introduced into their jobs, they emphasised the continuing relevance of their professional skills and knowledge for care management. As also shown in other studies (Davies and Connolly, 1995; Irving and Gertig, 1998; McGrath *et al.*, 1996; Rachman, 1995), a key concern among social workers was that they had less time for traditional casework tasks following the introduction of a more structured approach, focusing on the provision of practical assistance, coupled with a marked increase in the volume of referrals and the amount of associated paperwork to be completed.

The data on time use once more raises questions about the extent to which social workers are spending less time with service users. Other research suggests that face-to-face contact with clients has never accounted for more than about a third of social workers' time spent at work (Carver and Edwards, 1972; Law, 1982; Connor and Tibbitt, 1988). We have suggested that, irrespective of the actual duration of meetings, what may have changed is how client contact time is spent. The emphasis on completing the assessment process and arranging service packages means that there is less time available to undertake other activities such as providing emotional support.

The study also provides an insight into the similarities and differences in the jobs of hospital based and locality based social workers. The introduction of care management has imposed more uniformity on social work practice. One consequence of this is that the jobs undertaken by social workers in the two settings may be more similar now than before the 1993 changes.

Although the study showed that the range of tasks they undertook and the way in which they apportioned their time at work were broadly similar, there were important differences in the content of their jobs and in the pressures they experienced. Hospital social workers did not generally undertake long-term care management and review; rather, they transferred cases to locality teams after a specified period and this was reflected in their smaller caseloads. However, they felt under additional and different pressures compared with staff in locality based teams. These included working in a health care setting, fielding inappropriate referrals from medical and nursing staff and the faster turnover of the work partly due to demands from health professionals to expedite the discharge of patients. These findings underline the importance of adequate professional support for social services' staff working in health settings.

The study shows that hospital based social workers were more likely to report face-to-face contact with health professionals on their previous day at work, and to have spent more time in this way. The locality based social workers made more use of the telephone to communicate with health professionals but the majority had at least one contact with a health professional on their previous day at work. These findings highlight the increased opportunity for face-to-face contact with health when staff are based in a health setting, but the study was unable to provide any information on the content or quality of different types of contacts or on the adequacy and usefulness of the information exchanged. There is a clear need for further research to clarify these issues.

The finding that the majority of cases involved at least one health profession-al echoes other recent work (Manthorpe *et al.*, 1996; Petch *et al.*, 1996). The nature of this involvement varied. Many referrals originated from health pro-fessionals, health input was often sought during the assessment process, and service users with acute or chronic health problems required packages involving health service provision.

Many social workers in our study valued the increased scope for multidisci-plinary working in community care. As staff on the front line face the challenges arising from the more recent policy changes, questions are being raised about the future organisation of social work services. One possible model is total alignment with primary care. This reopens a longstanding debate as to whether or not the social care needs of hospital patients could be met by a locality based service, and whether the location of social workers in both primary and secondary care settings will always be required. Until now this debate has not been informed by systematic research that compares a range of different organisational arrangements and their outcomes for service users. This NISW study confirms that dealing with the interface with health already forms an important part of the working lives of social workers in both hospital and locality teams. It suggests that a better understanding of the cir-cumstances and conditions which facilitate good practice and positive outcomes for service users and carers may be as important as a focus on organisational arrangements. As one hospital social worker commented: 'Change does not necessarily mean major surgery each time.'

References

Balloch, S, McLean, J, and Fisher, M (eds) (1999) *Social Services: working under pressure* Bristol, Policy Press

Caldock, K (1994) 'Policy and practice: fundamental contradictions in the conceptualization of community care for elderly people?' *Health and Social Care in the Community* 2 (3), 133–141

Carver, V and Edwards, J L (1972) *Social Workers and their Workloads* London, National Institute for Social Work

Challis, D (1994) 'Care management' in Malin, N (ed) *Implementing Community Care* Buckingham, Open University Press

Challis, D (1998) Integrating health and social care: problems, opportunities and possibilities *Research, Policy and Planning* 16 (2), 7–12

Challis, D, Darton, R, Hughes, J, Stewart, K and Weiner, K (1998) *Care Management Study: Report on National Data* London, Department of Health

Connor, A and Tibbitt, J (1988) *Social Workers and Health Care in Hospitals* London, HMSO

Davies, M and Connolly, J (1995) 'Hospital social work and discharge planning: an exploratory study in East Anglia' *Health and Social Care in the Community* 3 (6),pp 363–371

DoH (Department of Health) (1989) *Caring for People: community care in the next decade and beyond* Cm 849, London, HMSO

DoH (Department of Health) (1998) *Modernising Social Services: promoting independence, improving protection, raising standards* Cm 4169, London, Stationery Office

Fisher, M (1991) 'Defining the practice content of care management' *Social Work and Social Sciences Review* 2 (3), pp 204–230

Goldberg, E M and Warburton, R W (1979) *Ends and Means in Social Work* London, George Allen and Unwin

Government Statistical Service (1996) *Key Indicators of Local Authority Social Services* London, Department of Health

Harding, T and Beresford, P (1996) *The Standards We Expect: what service users and carers want from social services workers* London, National Institute for Social Work

Higgins, R, Oldham, C and Hunter, DJ (1994) 'Working together: lessons for collaboration between health and social services' *Health and Social Care in the Community* 2 (5), pp 269–277

Hunter, D (1998) 'The new health policy agenda: the challenge facing managers and researchers' *Research, Policy and Planning* 16 (2), pp 2–6

Irving, J and Gertig, P (1998) 'Brave New World: social workers' perceptions of care management' *Practice* 10 (2), pp 5–14

La Valle, I and Lyons, K (1996) 'The social worker speaks: perceptions of recent changes in British social work' *Practice* 8 (2), pp 5–14

Law, E (1982) 'A light on hospital social work: a major study in Manchester' *Social Work Service* 29, pp 20–29

Lewis, J and Glennerster, H (1996) *Implementing the New Community Care* Buckingham, Open University Press

Lewis, R (1998) 'Change in social services', *Research, Policy and Planning* 16 (2), pp 13–15

LGMB (Local Government Management Board) (1997) *Social Services Workforce Analysis* 1996 Survey, London, LGMB

MacDonald, C (1999) *Support at Home – Views of Older People on their Needs and Access to Services* Edinburgh, Stationery Office

Manthorpe, J, Stanley, N, Bradley, G and Alaszewski, A (1996) 'Working together effectively? Assessing older people for community care services' *Health Care in Later Life* 1, pp 143–55

McGrath, M, Caldock, K, Grant, G, Parry-Jones, B, Ramcharan, P and Robinson, C (1996) 'The roles and tasks of care managers in Wales' *Community Care Management and Planning* 4 (6), pp 185–94

Moriarty, J and Webb, S (2000) *Part of their Lives: Community Care for Older People with Dementia* Bristol, Policy Press

Parsloe, P (1981) *Social Services Area Teams* London, George Allen and Unwin

Payne, M (1995) *Social Work and Community Care* London, Macmillan

Petch, A, Cheetham, J, Fuller, R, MacDonald, C, Myers, F with Hallam, A and Knapp, M (1996) *Delivering Community Care: Initial Implementation of Care Management in Scotland* Edinburgh, Stationery Office

Rachman, R (1995) 'Community Care: changing the role of hospital social work' *Health and Social Care in the Community* 3 (3), pp 163–172

Sheppard, M (1992) 'Contact and collaboration with general practitioners: a comparison of social workers and community psychiatric nurses' *British Journal of Social Work* 22 (4), pp 419–436

Sheppard, M (1995) *Care Management and the New Social Work: A Critical Analysis* London, Whiting and Birch

Sinclair, I, Parker, R, Leat, D and Williams, J (1990) *The Kaleidoscope of Care: A Review of Research on Welfare Provision for Elderly People* London, HMSO

Smale, G and Tuson, G (1993) *Empowerment, Assessment, Care Management and the Skilled Worker* London, HMSO

Smyth M (1996) *Qualified Social Workers and Probation Officers* London, Office for National Statistics

SSI (Social Services Inspectorate) (1998a) *Care Management Study – Care Management Arrangements* London, Department of Health

SSI (Social Services Inspectorate) (1998b) *Getting Better? Inspection of Hospital (Care Management) Arrangements for Older People* London, Department of Health

SSI/SWSG (Social Services Inspectorate/Scottish Office Social Work Services Group) (1991) *Care Management and Assessment: Practitioners' Guide*, London, HMSO

Standing Medical and Nursing & Midwifery Advisory Committees (1996) *In the Patient's Interest: multi-professional working across organisational boundaries* London, Department of Health

Tibbitt, J and Martin, P (1991) *Where the Time Goes* Edinburgh, The Scottish Office

Vanclay, L (1996) *Sustaining Collaboration between General Practitioners and Social Workers* London, Centre for the Advancement of Interprofessional Education (CAIPE)

Wistow, G (1994) 'Community care futures: interagency relationships – stability or continuing change?' in Titterton, M (ed) *Caring for People in the Community: the new welfare* London, Jessica Kingsley

Chapter 3
Care Management Across the Threshold

Jill Manthorpe and Greta Bradley

Introduction

This chapter presents research findings from a study of care management, focusing on social workers' management of health-related issues and their relationships with health service personnel. Social workers have been criticised for delaying assessment of older people in hospital, and this chapter explores the conflicting pressures to carry out proper assessment of need when individuals' circumstances and wishes are unclear and changing. First we consider the incorporation of hospital social work within the care management system. We explore the task of assessment, questioning the extent to which it represents a change or an extension to previous practice. Drawing on our research we consider professional pressures and complex issues of consent, capacity and trust. As might be expected, this chapter debates multidisciplinary working from the perspective of power and control. The extent to which care managers based in hospital settings are able to contribute to user-led assessment is explored together with their broader engagement with informal social networks. No discussion of social care and its borders with health services can escape the charging conundrum, and we point to the difficulties encountered by care managers who must discuss financial contributions at individual levels, often in emotionally charged circumstances, whilst under pressure from powerful players in the hospital system. We conclude with a picture of a group of social workers facing further changes.

The research described

This account draws on both quantitative data and material from 'shadowing' of the assessment process undertaken in hospital settings and in the community in a social services department in the North of England from 1994 to 1996. The research did not cover the whole of the care management process. Excluded from the study were issues concerning, for example, the targeting of potential service users, systems for implementing the care plan or the process of monitoring and review. Rather, the focus was on assessment in the context of the particular model of care management selected by the local authority concerned. Social services departments were given considerable latitude by central government in devising local structures for care management in its early days. Lewis and Glennerster (1996), for instance, have described the many variations of care management in their sample of local authorities. The department studied in our research had chosen to split the task of assessing people's needs from that of managing care packages. As a consequence separate posts had been created; those of assessors and those of coordinators. This research concentrated on the assessors since they had responsibility for the principal task of care management: that of assessment and putting together the care plan. Throughout this chapter we shall refer to these postholders as care managers since this term is more widely used in practice. There were 75 practitioners within this category, whose role was distinctive and well defined; this enabled the research team to take a close and focused look at the process of assessment.

When we approached senior managers in the department about our interest in exploring ways in which care managers were responding to the revised community care agenda, they were not immediately receptive. They were interested in research which had direct relevance to practice and which had an obvious feedback loop into the work of the agency (Bradley, 1997). Following discussion it became apparent that the department wished to sponsor a quantitative study to explore the extent to which the training of this large group of practitioners had been effective. This complemented our interests in the wider attitudinal shifts of the new culture of care management. Thus we were able to demonstrate to senior officers in the department that there were large areas of overlapping interest between their interests and ours. For example, both parties wanted to discover the extent to which the recently appointed staff in care management had embraced the new culture of community care, given that, with one exception, all of those involved in this task were social work trained (98.5 per cent). A key focus was the extent to which the care managers were drawing on traditional social work skills and whether new skills were being developed. However, the commissioners saw the research more in terms of the agency's goals. They were interested in whether the care managers were familiar with the authority's objectives in community care and if the initial training for the new job had been both useful and effective.

Given the differences in perspective, a steering group was established including 'stakeholders' from the department at senior and middle management levels, from training and from practice in the field of adult services. The steering group was a great asset to the research. For example, the 93 per cent response rate to the questionnaire was aided by the way it was promoted enthusiastically by team leaders who had been well briefed by their line managers as a consequence of the department supporting and promoting the research.

The research was multifaceted and included a survey, interviews and a shadowing exercise. All care managers (75) in hospital and community settings were sent a six-page questionnaire which was mainly in the form of a 'tick-box' to enhance the likelihood of replies. Details concerning professional experience, formal qualifications and future career aspirations were requested. The questionnaire was anonymised to establish a clear boundary between the department and the research team. It was posted independently to the care managers and included a stamped addressed envelope for direct return. Additionally, all direct line managers (23 in total) and four senior managers with responsibility for care management in adult services were interviewed by telephone to explore their views about the recent changes and the challenges arising (Stanley, 1999).

To compliment these data ten cases were shadowed which fitted the criteria for a full community care assessment. All elements of the assessment process from the initial allocation to the care manager to the final meeting with the service user were observed. With the permission of the service user and family members, as appropriate, we observed, tape-recorded and took notes of encounters with primarily social services staff. This was followed by debriefing discussions with the care manager. Copies of the completed Community Care Assessment forms were examined in order to compare material from the taped interviews and the outcome of the care plan. This research technique enabled us to view practice at close quarters. For example, we were able to hear the ways in which the needs and aspirations of users were elicited and recorded. This included close scrutiny of the process of assessment such as the techniques for obtaining consent, particularly informed consent when a user's mental capacity was in doubt. We were also able to observe when and why a specialist assessment or a specialist service was accessed.

Out of a possible 75 care managers 69 replied, 19 of whom were hospital based, representing 27.5 per cent of the respondents. For the purposes of these discussions material relating to the 19 hospital based care managers is specifically explored, unless a comparison between settings is illuminating (for a fuller description of the methodology see Stanley *et al.*, 1998). These 19 care managers had been known as hospital social workers until the reforms. However, the place of hospital social work in the new organisational structures had been left comparatively unchanged following the implementation of the community care reforms. Far more energy had been expended on community based care managers' geographical location and their managerial relationships. The focus on contracts, costings and revised relationships with the Benefits Agency and the independent sector, meant concentrating on those working with people in the community. Regarded as generally sound and unproblematic, hospital social work was expected to continue much as usual.

Three of the ten care managers shadowed in this research were based in hospital settings. One care manager was attached to a surgical ward within a hospital that served a predominantly rural community in a shire county; a second was attached to a medical ward in a small district general hospital located in a community with an urban core within a rural hinterland; the third was based on a ward for older people within a general hospital that served an urban community with a high level of deprivation. The following discussion considers the shift from hospital social work to the new work of care management experienced by these practitioners.

From hospital social worker to care manager

The evaluation of early care management experimental projects revealed that care management entailed a continuation of much that was evident in hospital social work. The Darlington Community Care project (Challis *et al.*, 1995), for example, illustrated that terms such as case finding and screening were common aspects of case conferences, ward meetings and informal referral patterns. This process consisted of informal discussions, consensus views and convenient meetings. Visits were made to patients on the wards and home visits were sometimes attended by a variety of professionals. In this way assessments were built up. By the time of the first case conference much initial work had been done. The social worker could then concentrate on:

- making the service acceptable
- balancing client and carer needs
- managing acceptable levels of risk
- acting as an advocate
- balancing needs, demands and scarcity (pp.77–80).

Much of this appeared familiar territory to hospital based social workers. It is inevitable that people who meet the criteria for community care assessment have complex needs. Some of these needs may have been brought to the attention of the statutory services for the first time by the extensive process of assessment in hospital. These needs may be of a health, personal, social and/or financial nature and may require a limited encounter with the care manager. Time to clarify feelings and issues within a helping relationship may be all that is needed. Alternatively, more discussion may be appropriate to consider issues and feelings of a deeper nature or to make significant decisions. This work may involve the use of counselling skills. Scrutton (1999) provides a definition of counselling peculiarly appropriate to hospital social work when he describes it as a process which is about 'facing pain and empathising with it' (p.5). It has been customary to assume that hospital social workers drew on such skills in their day-to-day work. Helping people to adjust to loss or to major life changes, for example, as a consequence of a physical trauma, acute ill-health or serious disability, has been one of the hallmarks of hospital social work, at least in those settings studied (Connor and Tibbett, 1988; Rachman, 1995). We must be careful, however, not to exaggerate these claims, since many studies of hospital social work have been based on work in specialist and prestigious fields such as regional hospital units for younger people.

Despite this it was apparent from the results of the survey that the overwhelming majority (18) of hospital based care managers in our study (95 per cent) saw counselling an essential skill. Thirteen agreed or strongly agreed (68 per cent) that they were able to use their therapeutic or counselling skills in the process of their work. In contrast, only 36 per cent of those working in the community said they were able to use such skills. This confirms the findings of Lewis and Glennerster (1996). They noted that locality based care managers in their study awarded more time to practical tasks than to counselling and that for them the balance of work had 'swung firmly away from counselling' (p.140). Indeed, other research (Davies and Connelly 1995) has suggested that hospital staff did not require or need hospital based social workers to undertake counselling. However, Rachman's (1995) research on the role of hospital social work following the implementation of the community care reforms confirmed our finding that counselling was still perceived by care managers as an integral part of their work. Whilst hospital social workers in one of the four authorities in her study were 'struggling to retain the counselling component' of their work, in other authorities, particularly in specialist hospital units, social workers continued to regard counselling as central to their role (p.166).

Nonetheless, when the day-to-day activity of hospital based care managers became the object of study as part of the shadowing exercise, it became clear that the place of counselling within such a setting was becoming more proscribed. When faced with other pressures, the care managers were less certain of their counselling role even though they may have thought it a 'good thing'. As one care manager reflected:

I'm not sure about the counselling bit – it depends how you define counselling . . . I can't spend as much time as I would like – as I used to. On my first visit I hear them out, give them the time they need, then after that I try to negotiate my way, bring them back to the forms.

This statement also reflects how the assessment forms were being used effectively to construct the assessment into a dialogue, but such a dialogue was not considered to be counselling.

Old wine in new bottles? The work of assessment
People in hospital who are eligible for a Community Care Assessment are likely to have interrelated problems of both a health and a social nature. Prior to 1993 it was possible that hospital social workers would have had the time to help patients in a similar position to clarify their attitudes and feelings and follow through the work as necessary (Rachman, 1995). With the increased administrative, liaison and coordinating roles imposed on care managers in hospitals, research suggests that this interpersonal aspect of their work is curtailed (Caldock and Nolan, 1994). This shift is seen as a general trend in care management. Phillips (1996) argued:

> Social work practice has moved from a service orientated approach to one of assessment of individual need and care management embodying
>
> principles of empowerment and choice; however the interpersonal elements of social work including the important therapeutic relationship have been reduced with, instead, a greater emphasis placed on the management of cases. (p.136)

The completion of the Community Care Assessment form has become a highly focused and time-consuming activity. Most forms are likely to be at least 15 pages in length and frequently require the consent of the service user to trigger related assessments by other professionals. When these were first introduced, the Department of Health (DoH, SSI, SO, SWSG, 1991) guidance promoted timely and focused assessments based on a 'need to know' principle (p.58). More recent practice guidance (Middleton, 1997, p.67) suggested that a good assessment whilst 'collecting only relevant data' also:

- starts with an open mind
- involves and empowers the user as a partner
- explores the pros and cons of a range of solutions
- does not put pressure on the user to choose the options the assessor wants
- negotiates with the individual, and with existing and potential service providers, to find an acceptable and feasible solution.

However, this research identified both the forms and associated administrative procedures as significant hurdles to such empowering practice. This was apparent in the quantitative study and in our observations of the communication and behaviour of care managers in the presence of service users. In the question-naire care managers described the forms as 'off-putting', 'constraining', 'repetitive' and 'voluminous'. Other research on social work practice records that report writing and the completion of forms are amongst the most time-consuming activities for field social workers as well (Balloch, McLean and Fisher, 1999, p.52).

Professional pressure
In the shadowing exercise a hospital based care manager commented that the new role felt like a 'stressful balancing act'. He explained:

> *there were increasingly more assessments to be done with pressure to deliver within a short space of time and I would be dishonest to say that we do not respond to the pressure to empty beds – but only up to a point*

In his view, hospital based care managers were pulled in two directions: 'knowing how expensive it is to keep a person in hospital to being sensitive to the need, particularly of elderly people, to give them time to make up their minds.'

Pressure emanating from the 'bed clearing' priorities experienced in all hospital sites was compounded by administrative pressures imposed on hospital based care managers. In the postal survey, 17 (89 per cent) of the hospital based care managers agreed (and 12 of these strongly so) that they spent too much time filling in forms. However, when shadowing this group of care managers, we observed that they used the forms in different ways, for example, as a tool to 'get things done' or for 'steering' the interview. Practitioners frequently referred to the forms in their first meeting with the service user. Here they obtained the necessary signatures, took the occasional note and completed large sections away from the service user and the ward. Taking the forms home in the evenings to input data away from the noise of the office was also a common practice. Whilst the care managers generally kept the forms 'at arm's length' metaphori-cally, it was noticeable that they were used as a mechanism of control. For example, one care manager referred to them when she wanted to refocus the interview and draw it back from areas which she had designated less important. The following description of a meeting between Mrs Walker, a patient in her late eighties recovering from a fall, and the care manager illustrates this:

> In her first conversation, the care manager established that Mrs Walker did not wish to return home but rather to enter the residential accommodation where her husband had died. On the basis of this brief conversation the care manager decided on a full Community Care Assessment and returned the following day with the forms. When her husband and daughters were

mentioned in conversation, Mrs Walker became quite emotional and her eyes filled with tears. The care manager chose not to explore these feelings in any detail but in a manner which was both sympathetic and yet firm, she steered the conversation back to the assessment, enquiring who was in possession of the bank books and requesting permission for a financial assessment. When discussing how she managed before the accident, Mrs Walker responded emotionally, 'I feel so weary, I just want to lay back and go to sleep.' The care manager responded to this disclosure in a gentle manner but she manoeuvred the conversation back to financial matters and issues concerning the tenancy arrangements of the council property, which linked back to a section on the forms.

On another occasion, when a care manager in another hospital was conducting an assessment with Mrs Adams, a patient on the ward, he forgot to take the assessment forms with him and he broke off the interview to collect them from his office. It was noticeable that when he returned with the forms he was much more focused in his approach. Mrs Adams, who was in her early eighties and lived alone in sheltered housing, had been admitted with a complex fracture. She appeared to need support such as respite accommodation before returning home. Much of the interview was taken up by the care manager explaining the assessment form and the nature of the consent required. He described the process of assessment in some detail, using language which was straightforward and accessible. With reference to the eligibility criteria he explained: 'there are certain bands in which people are placed depending on their needs and these bands trigger a service.'

Thus it is not simply a matter of form-filling taking up time for it can be managed by practitioners in a variety of ways. The forms can dominate the conversation and be visible illustrations of bureaucracy: a worker lacking in confidence can almost hide behind the paperwork. Alternatively, they can convey to service users that there is some equity and respect for their views and circumstances. This may be particularly important in the potentially disempowering settings of hospital wards where the status of patient assumes a dependency and deference to expert medical opinion. We explore below issues that arise when seeking users' views.

Consent, capacity and trust
Whilst the majority of hospital based care managers saw extensive form-filling and obtaining signatures as bureaucratic hurdles, these pressures also generated areas of difficulties in decision-making in relationship to informed consent and mental capacity. It was noticeable in the shadowing that because

workers had related the forms to the process of assessment with the service user, it appeared an easy step to refer back to them to explain the nature of consent. When discussing this issue with Mrs Adams, the care manager, in a matter-of-fact and yet apparently sincere manner, said: 'I need your consent before I can contact other people or agencies on your behalf to give information I need to do the assessment.' At another point in the conversation the care manager stated that: 'I need to be happy that you know what you are doing.'

In the process of setting up the respite accommodation the care manager explained that he would eventually need Mrs Adams's signature, but before this point he would need to check her level of payment and benefit allowance with both the Department of Social Security and the Social Services Finance Officer. 'Oh' said Mrs Adams, 'I'll sign them now, I trust you'. This seemed a genuine response and indicated to the researcher that whilst quite functional conversation had taken place within the interview, the care manager had established a sound working relationship which also conveyed some basic principles of good practice. In a debriefing interview afterwards the care manager nonetheless reflected that he wanted to give service users as much time as possible to make up their mind: 'I'll probably go through the finances again with Mrs Adams, there was a lot to take in'.

In a debriefing session some days later the care manager admitted that the whole process of consent worried him:

It's pretty obvious when a person is very confused and if there is a relative we have to rely on the relative's signature, but I do almost every other day wonder how much on earth the client has understood what I'm on about and what they're signing for. I try to explain it but sometimes it's too much, honestly.

The recent proposals from the Lord Chancellor's Department in *A Charter for Carers* (1999) may help clarify decision-making processes when capacity is impaired, but for many care managers in hospital settings some levels of confusion and disorientation appear to be relatively common among patients, if temporary. Even if the new proposals are implemented there will be still many people whose capacity is clouded but not impaired: the problem of involving them fully in decisions is unlikely to pass completely. If hospital social workers are to represent the views and interests of individual patients they must know what these are. Weak indication of this may cause difficulties in multidisciplinary forums.

New powers? Multidisciplinary working
All the care managers in this study were asked about their communication with staff from health services, both in hospitals and in the community. In order to

go beyond generalities the respondents were asked to focus on their last ten assessments, which were likely to be better remembered and fairly representative. One-quarter of care managers said they had contacted hospital consultants (such as geriatricians or surgeons) or registrars in each of their ten last assessments, while another quarter had liaised with hospital doctors concerning between four and seven of their last ten assessments. As expected, the care managers in the study who had made such contact were predominantly hospital based. There was a tendency for hospital based care managers to seek information mainly from doctors whom they knew and saw frequently in connection with service users/patients currently in hospital and with whom they were professionally involved. The precise patterning of multidisciplinary contact is both individually constructed and also a product of team and agency relationship. We found that even within one local authority there were differences in the roles of teams, both within social services and in respect of 'client group' specialisms. This means that guidance from the Department of Health about multidisciplinary working has to be applied to widely varying situations.

Multidisciplinary work, of course, is not a new concept. Indeed, it has been a guiding principle of health related social work throughout its history. Government directives and working papers over the past 30 years have extolled the virtues of 'working together'. One of the standards developed by the Social Services Inspectorate (1999) in its exploration of social services departments' links with primary health services for older people was that arrangements should be made to define 'their respective roles and responsibilities in arrangements for hospital admissions and hospital discharge arrangements' (p.32). According to Caldock (1996) a key objective of multidisciplinary work must be 'to provide a service in which the boundaries between primary health, secondary health care and social care do not form barriers seen from the perspective of the care user' (p.34). She argued, nonetheless, that in a culture of social care, which promotes interagency competition within a budget conscious market, the incentives for key agencies to collaborate have been challenged. The mixed economy of care she considered played its part in undermining interprofessional relations, since without adequate funding, one professional group would be reluctant, not surprisingly, to accept responsibility for social care services. Indeed, Davies and Connelly (1995) found that some hospital professionals considered social workers 'aloof' and removed from the practicalities of care and the juggling of scarce resources which enabled them to claim the 'moral high ground' (p.306).

Such problems between the boundaries of acute hospital and community care services are not confined to the UK. Glendinning (1998) described a common international pattern of tighter acute boundaries producing coordination

problems around prevention of admission and facilitation of early discharges. Integrated domiciliary teams providing nursing and personal care
services are seen as the way forward in many areas. Other initiatives, such as
those developed in Australia (Howe, 1997) have prompted development of
financial incentives around discharge packages.

The role of care managers in hospitals with power to set up care plans
suggests that compared with former hospital social workers, they have more
influence over when a patient is discharged and this affects the power balance
with medical colleagues. They are the ones with responsibility for undertaking community care assessments, to take or convey decisions over funding
and put the care package into place before the discharge is finally arranged.
One of the care managers in the shadowing exercise definitely thought he
now had more power and professional control: as a consequence he felt he
was able to be more assertive:

> *(I) . . . can't stay in the back seat like I used to since nothing would get
> done – got to be more proactive – it's more stressful.*

These sentiments were echoed in the responses to the survey. The great
majority (95 per cent) of hospital based care managers said that they thought
negotiation was an essential skill in their work. Another care manager, when
asked if the role had affected her relationship with medical and ward staff,
responded:

> *Yes there has been a different form of conflict, I think it's because we
> have more power in our role, we are more an intricate part of a
> discharge policy. Before we were seen as less important in the consul-
> tant's eyes. Now we've been put in the front line and if we don't do our
> assessment, that person will not be discharged. We're more account-
> able and it has affected our role. There is more conflict with the
> consultants. We were right at the bottom, but now because we have
> more statutory involvement they have to accept our view.*

Liaison with all hospital based staff, such as doctors, nurses and, occasional-
ly, occupational therapists and physiotherapists appeared to be immensely
varied. It seemed reliant on a combination of personalities, organisational
practices and culture. Relationships with hospital staff were often seen on an
individual basis. Care managers identified some doctors and nurses as
'helpful' and others as 'unhelpful'. Those care managers who had been
working in a hospital for some time had a clear idea of who could be relied on
to produce information that was accurate, relevant and nonjudgemental. The
converse was also true. The history of Mrs Walker, who had fractured her hip

after a fall and was discussed earlier, (page 77) illustrates this. The medical report to the care manager simply stated: 'Admitted on (date) with fractured neck of left femur, operated on (date), mobilising with frame, think would need residential care'. This care manager told us that in her experience many reports were even more cursory and some were not completed.

The observational methodology permitted an exploration of the way in which care managers responded to such reports when they perceived a need for further information: in this case, details of Mrs Walker's prognosis, possible level of functioning and needs, as opposed to a 'prescription' for residential care. In this case the care manager was observed tackling the difficulty not precisely 'in a spirit of pragmatic co-operation' to use the Department of Health's term (DoH, SSI, 1993, p.1), but in a spirit of pragmatic compensation. She did this by locating a more 'helpful' informant, in this instance the ward staff nurse. The care manager then talked to the nurse in a room off the ward and made notes to help her to complete her assessment form with the medical information required. Following this, the care manager kept herself up to date by visiting the ward and talking to Mrs Walker's named nurse (the nurse allocated to the patient, who would have responsibility for overseeing nursing care). There was no further contact with the doctor and no ward mechanism for sending reports on Mrs Walker's changing condition to the care manager.

Compensation or the development of 'alternative' sources of information could also help care managers if they found conflicts among other professionals. In the situation of Mrs Adams, for example, the care manager was told by the medical registrar that the patient would need a month in residential care for rehabilitation. However, the named nurse challenged this since she thought that Mrs Adams could manage, with help, at home. The nurse commented: 'Registrars know nothing about the real world.' In order to deal with these conflicting opinions, the care manager sought another view: that of the occupational therapist. The latter commented that doctors gave limited information and many of them had little knowledge about nursing or residential homes, despite recommending them. The occupational therapist supported the nurse's view.

Our observations indicated that named nurses played a key role. They were often seen as key informants because they possessed a relatively sophisticated knowledge of the patient's behaviour, emotional state and medical prognosis. They acquired this through their own interactions with patients but also by virtue of their coordinating role, which gave them access to round-the-clock observation. The coordinating functions of the care manager were parallel to their own. This made assessment within hospitals often procedurally easier, although the patient's changing condition and, frequently, the severity of the illness could draw out the assessment process. This potential alliance of care managers and nurses develops both into formidable allies, particularly if they pride themselves on being patient advocates (Manthorpe *et al.*, 1996).

Missed opportunities in power sharing

It would be disingenuous to suggest that care management has totally redirected power to social services. As the research of Stanley, Reed and Brown (1999) discovered, the hospital may still be a metaphorical 'battleground' for conflict.

> There was clear evidence from the interviews that the moving of the patient/client along the hospital admission/discharge through to the care home or home was characterised by a certain amount of interprofessional rivalry (p.234).

In their study, some professionals talked of 'patrolling' (p.235) the boundaries of health and social care to ensure they were not breached and no health care staff member had experience of interprofessional training. In their view the health arena was still 'hierarchically conscious' and the concept of care management did not fit well with established understandings of hospital leadership.

Some of the observational data from our research confirmed this insight. For example, we shadowed a hospital based care manager chairing a multidisciplinary case conference. Afterwards, she reflected that she had not used her new powers in the role of care manager to full advantage. Neither, she admitted, had she embraced some of the basic tenets of power sharing, particularly with service users and their families. A description of this case conference held about Mr Jones (a single man in his late fifties referred for assessment following major surgery which had increased his disability) illustrates these points:

> There were twelve participants at the case conference including Mr Jones and five members of his family, the care manager and two social services staff from the area, a physiotherapist, an occupational therapist and a nurse from the ward. As an introduction, the care manager emphasised the importance of finding acceptable solutions to meet the service user's needs. She stressed that all conference members needed to be actively involved, but particularly the family and the local social services staff since this partnership was particularly important. As soon as the meeting started, the care manager turned to the three hospital based staff and asked

for their views. She justified this by explaining that two of them had to leave early. During the following thirty five minutes the meeting virtually excluded the service user and his family. A 'deficit list' had been compiled by the ward staff for the meeting. These were areas where Mr Jones required help and which were problematic. This was complemented by a 'demand chart' which itemised the number of his 'night time inter-ruptions' and the level of attention requested during the night. The main carer interrupted once saying that it would be different when his brother returned home. The ward staff were not receptive to this point of view; it appeared that they thought it important that family members did not go away with a false impression of Mr Jones' coping abilities. This 'deficit' model of Mr Jones' profile was not challenged by the care manager, neither was support given to the family who appeared to have difficulties elaborating an alternative point of view. Hospital staff also emphasised that they would have no further responsibility for Mr Jones once the discharge arrangements were finalised. Social services staff were then invited to speak. They said that they would see how Mr Jones coped at home and that they would interpret the care plan as they saw fit and as resources allowed.

It seemed that the care manager had little room to negotiate in these circum-stances. She appeared caught between the intransigent opinion of the hospital staff that high levels of care would be required at home and the equally firm opinion of the care providers and family that they would see what happened once he had gone home. What could be perceived as a strong negotiating position, as chair of the meeting and designated care manager, quickly dissipat-ed. Initially, when interviewed immediately after the meeting, the care manager appeared surprised that the order in which people were invited to speak was perceived to be relevant. She said that it was 'custom and practice' for busy hospital staff to speak first and that for two colleagues there was a clear rationale. She was quick to accept nonetheless the message which this gave to Mr Jones and his family and how this affected the power balance of the meeting, helping to reinforce the differential between professionals, service users and their families. She also reflected that she felt to be in the middle of two different professional cultures and that her role was less that of power broker than go-between. This is a common if underarticulated theme in hospital social work. Regarded by hospital staff as not one of them, such prac-titioners may be perceived by social service colleagues as colluding over-much with medical or nursing professionals. User-led assessment is hard to maintain in the face of other demands, as we discuss below.

User-led assessment?
Respecting the wishes of users is a key element of an empowering service. One of the three key aims of the White Paper *Caring for People* was to 'give people a greater individual say in how they run their lives and the services they need to help them do so' (Secretaries of State for Health, 1989, sect. 1.8). In the case of Mrs Walker, the care manager appeared to be operating a 'procedural model' of care management (Smale *et a*l., 1993), interpreting the facts within administrative boundaries whilst at the same time attempting to keep the assessment user-led. The research team described the case of Mrs Walker as predominantly user-led since the care manager had accepted virtually without question her preference to be admitted from the medical ward to a residential home, as we mentioned earlier (p. 77). The underlying assumption was that the service user knew what was best for her, even in the face of information which could have suggested otherwise. For example, when Mrs Walker explained why she could no longer live at home, her reasoning mainly centred around loneliness: 'I'm not frightened but just a little nervy about being left on my own.'

When Mrs Walker suggested that after a period of recovery she could re-establish her relatively active life, the care manager passed over this:

Care Manager: Were you managing OK before the death of your husband and before the fall at home?

Mrs Walker: Oh definitely.

Care Manager: It's obviously knocked you back, hasn't it?

Mrs Walker: Oh definitely.

O'Sullivan (1999) illustrated the pressure on older people to 'opt' for residential care by their focusing on the least bad alternative. Writing about the case of a Mr Smith, O'Sullivan observed:

> he exaggerates the good points and ignores the disadvantages of the least objectionable course of action and so avoids systematically examining the options. For Mr Smith, the least objectionable alternative is moving to residential care and so he minimises the losses involved in giving up his home and emphasises the advantages of residential care (1999, p.100).

In a climate of consent and partnership replacing paternalism, care managers may need to develop their practice in assisting users with their decision-making over residential care. One of the most significant implications of 'prejudged' referrals for residential and nursing home care is that by the time assessment is started, older people and their carers are often resigned to the belief that a return home is no longer possible (Stevenson, 1999, p.8). The care manager in our study did not consider the disadvantages of a permanent residential placement for Mrs Walker. When questioned by the researcher, the care manager gave a pragmatic answer explaining that even though a short-term placement might have been more appropriate she had been advised by the social services Finance Office to seek a permanent residential placement. Mrs Walker was deemed to be eligible for higher benefits if this approach was taken. The care manager also said that if a placement had to be converted from a short to a permanent placement it would entail more form-filling. However, under further questioning she justified the approach in terms of Mrs Walker's interest. The care manager saw herself as user-centred since she enabled Mrs Walker to enter the home she wished and to spend her own money as she chose on the costs of this care. When asked what would happen if Mrs Walker were admitted as a permanent resident but then made a full recovery within a short period, the care manager replied:

> *I really struggle with this . . . I accept the fact that there might be misuse of resources, but I think people still should have a choice. . . yes she's border-line . . . but she doesn't want to return home, that for me is the main thing.*

When asked if the department would then continue to pay the costs when Mrs Walker's own savings fell below the threshold for payment of residential care, the care manager replied:

> *I don't think any worker would overturn the decision when the money ran out, since it would not be compassionate or human to turn someone away from where they want to be. At the end of the day we're here for people.*

Such important decisions were made in the early days of Mrs Walker's hospital stay, that is even before the care manager made enquiries about her progress from the ward staff or medical personnel. She was taking an advocacy or user-led approach in which she represented the service user in the face of official approaches from both health and social services. Such independence may be more feasible for those based at some distance from mainstream social work services and management. We found that hospital care managers had some status in arguing that their service users were in need. There was general acceptance that given the shortage of hospital beds, those with the key to unlock apparent discharge delays were given great credence in contrast to those arguing that individuals should have their stay extended on the ward. One important characteristic of the hospital social worker is his or her ability to act in a world outside the hospital. While this may not always be evident or needed, it most firmly applies to work with social networks where the hospital social worker has a valid and accepted role in going beyond the hospital, and we move to this point below.

Hospital discharge and social networks

While much emphasis has been placed in recent years on working with and supporting carers in the community and delivery of care packages, hospital social workers also recognise wider support networks in their assessment. The work of Wenger and her colleagues (1994) has been useful in drawing attention to the variations in social support networks existing among older people and their implications for practice. Based on a longitudinal study of older people in North Wales, Wenger illustrated the impact of different network types on service provision around hospital discharge. Wenger identified a number of typical 'networks' and explored their implications for decision-making.

For individuals with networks that are *local family dependent*, typically a person living with a spouse or relative and with other family support, Wenger showed that such individuals would often return home from hospital with complex and difficult needs, but that families would be both welcoming and prepared. She suggested that services may need to be long-term as the level of need, say for nursing care, could be quite high. Carers would themselves benefit from monitoring and increases in support as the situation developed. It would appear that hospital social workers in such cases need to balance everyone's enthusiasm for a rapid hospital discharge by ensuring that carers have sustained support through a regularly monitored package of care, if appropriate.

For the second model 'type' of support networks, Wenger (1994) identified people whose networks are *locally integrated*, a broader range of family, friends and neighbours providing practical and emotional support. They too appear likely to facilitate earlier hospital discharge, and care tasks may be shared between them. Wenger envisaged more need for reassurance among this network, and again a possible call on specialised services to provide discrete aspects of nursing care. Mr Jones, one of the cases shadowed, fitted well with this model since his networks were locally integrated and he relied heavily on informal support for his home based care. Mr Jones had a large family, with several siblings at or near retirement age like himself, and many nephews and nieces. He was also well known in his community since he had been very sociable when in better health and these links were sustained. Even though he had a high level of disability on leaving hospital, his friends and relatives attempted to maintain as normal a life as possible for him. However, relatives who were offering a high level of support following discharge quickly began to realise that demands were high on the family and friends. One of Mr Jones's sisters had worked in a residential home and she was able to assess the type of care that her brother needed. She began to argue that her brother might be more suitable for residential care, since her professional view was that too much of the care was falling to their brother who shared the house with Mr Jones.

Both such networks generally provide high levels of support and account for many of the instances where there is little or no social services involvement in patients' assessments. Ward staff may classify such patients as not in need of social services' attention: particularly when social work teams are stretched. It is easy to forget that most older people in hospital do not come to the attention of the social work team.

Wenger's other model types, however, may represent the circumstances of people who cross the referral threshold. Those individuals with *local self-contained networks* are typically those with supportive neighbours but family members who live some distance away. Here help may be available on a short-term basis from relatives, and neighbours may 'keep an eye on' or monitor the situation. However, it may be that the older person returns home to an empty, even cold or unprovisioned home. Domiciliary help in the form of 'home help' cleaning, meal preparation and personal assistance may be warranted. For many social workers the lack of a reliable, flexible, rapid response has been frustrating. Various innovative short-term projects continue to prove the need for such responses but, like much special project work, often appear to be terminating before they are fully utilised.

For those with networks that are *wider community focused* a typical pattern might be that friends form the prominent source of help while family members live some distance away. Geography does not mean that such individuals do not receive any help from relatives, but again this is likely to be short-term or con- centrated on times such as hospital discharge. While friends may provide assistance at a number of levels, Wenger cautioned that they may withdraw if too great demands are made: investment in practical help may 'prop up' such friends (and for older people such friends are highly likely to be older people them- selves, with poor or variable health) allowing them to continue to provide emotional and social supports. The current emphasis on prevention may serve to justify some additional resources to support such networks. Mrs Adams and her relatives (described on page 78) fitted this model since she would have to rely heavily on her immediate family on leaving hospital. Whilst her daughter-in-law was 'welcoming' she also displayed a high level of anxiety about the extent of commitment involved. Perceptions of coping capacity can differ markedly between carers and service users. There may be complex reasons why some service users describe their competence in positive ways, particularly if they perceive that discharge arrangements may be affected. When Mrs Adams, a widow of several years living in sheltered housing and intent on an early return home, was asked how she would cope given her fractured arm, she described herself as 'very easy going'. Her daughter-in-law visibly bridled at this description and said that her mother-in-law was 'Obsessed with washing and cleaning and couldn't bear to see anything untidy.'

Her daughter-in-law seemed alarmed by the 'I can cope' message being projected, in the knowledge of the pressures on her to respond to her mother-in-law's expectations of household cleanliness. This alarm may also have reflected her own inability to provide sustained help due to the geographical distance. There could also be other agendas not known to the care manager. Within the confines of a hospital ward and a time-limited assessment interview, as hospital social workers have always appreciated, it may be difficult to judge where exactly reality lies.

Wenger's final 'model' type, networks which are *private restricted*, often resonates with social workers in practice since this form of network seems likely to lead to both initial referrals to social services and then a range of complex negotiations. Such networks, as the name suggests, are found among people who might be termed 'loners' or socially isolated. Individuals have small numbers within their social circles; family, if any, may live at a distance or be estranged. On discharge from hospital a number of concerns by professionals may surface: the home may appear unsuitable, there may be anxiety about levels of self-care or issues of self-neglect and the individual may refuse or curtail services. Such individuals may be seen as 'suitable' or 'eligible' for residential care: however, this form of communal, institutional life may be anathema to them.

Wenger's ideal types or models provide a useful framework for discussions of hospital based care managers' understanding of and engagement with support networks. This chapter continues with illustrations of some of the themes she has raised. It is an area of research that is highly relevant to practice and one which may be placed under further scrutiny in the context of new emphases on prevention, particularly if prevention is seen as preventing breakdown among caring networks rather than narrowly defined as preventing of illness or frailty.

Carers as active participants in the discharge process

The role of hospital based care managers as advocates may involve the promotion of the interests of users, but also of carers. Nolan, Grant and Keady (1996) have drawn attention to the temptation for hospital staff to assume that the presence of a relative means that intensive informal care is available:

Within the present climate of ever more rapid hospital discharge, the time available for both carers and cared-for persons to make important decisions about future care options is diminishing. It seems increasingly likely that growing numbers of carers will adopt the role without adequate thought, advice and preparation (p.48).

Nolan *et al.*, developed the idea that periods of hospitalisation exacerbate certain pressures and problems within care systems. They noted, for example, that 'the onus is placed on the carer to be the prime mover' (p.127). The 'patient' may be too ill or confused to make decisions or to be consulted properly. This pressure is hurried as beds are universally accepted to be valuable and in short supply. However, 'with few exceptions carers received minimal help at this difficult period' (p.128), leaving many relatives with enduring senses of guilt or stress. Adequate professional assistance at that time, help with decision-making and emotional preparation, were unfortunately not commonly reported by carers. This is despite government guidance that the needs of carers of vulnerable people leaving hospital must be an integral part of the discharge arrangements, for example, the Department of Health (DoH, 1989) circular on *Discharge of Patients from Hospital*.

Hospital based care managers in this research were more likely to identify issues amongst carers than their colleagues in the community; 38 per cent said that they quite often experienced conflict between carers and users, compared with 28 per cent of care managers based in the community. Hospital admission may bring matters to a head, as the case of Mr Jones illustrated (see pages 83 and 87). His sister appeared to see matters differently after the hospital admission which had provided some respite for his family. In other circumstances, admissions may provide an opportunity to 'take stock' and to alter arrangements which are becoming unsustainable. Many hospital social workers recalled the days when hospital admission was used for respite purposes, providing families with guaranteed periods when their relatives could be cared for or assessed on medical grounds and often referred to these as 'social admissions'.

A recent qualitative study by Heaton and colleagues (1999) examined carers' experiences of hospital discharge and continuing care arrangements of younger adults with complex needs and physical disabilities. They identified a tension between a needs-led philosophy and service-based provision. This was evident in the 'lack of real choice made available to carers' (p 97). Carers would have liked to have had a clearer idea of the choices available to them; in particular whether there were alternatives to their caring role. Again this was evident in the care provided to Mr Jones. He and his relatives were told by the community care providers to 'wait and see' how he responded to his immediate discharge home before the care package was given shape. Heaton *et al.*, also raised the important point of whether the views of carers should be elicited independently. In our study, Mr Jones's brother was interviewed independently but only briefly. The survey undertaken as part of this study indicated that 40 per cent of hospital based care managers had completed a carer's assessment in the preceding three months. This contrasted with community based care managers of whom 73 per cent had completed such an assessment. Heaton *et al.*, similarly drew attention to the fact that the Carers (Recognition and Services) Act 1995 was making slow impact on discharge planning arrangements and the needs of carers (see also Carers National Association, 1997 and Carers National Association/Association of Directors of Social Work/Association of Directors of Social Services,1997).

Heaton *et al.*, called for hospital discharge practice to be 'cross-referenced' with the Carers' Act and, for example, to incorporate a protocol for informing carers of their rights to an assessment at the time, providing they fulfil the criteria. They argued that too much emphasis was placed on the needs of the patient. This led to:

> lack of clarity and parity in policy regarding the respective rights of patients and carers in discharge planning, it was reflected in the patient-focussed nature of the discharge practices . . . whilst carers' needs were rarely overlooked completely, patients' views tended to take priority' (p.98).

Patients' circumstances can appear pre-eminent and enquiries into these may have been further complicated by financial assessment. Means-testing is a contentious area, as we discuss below.

Paying for services
While patients' views were important, all care managers operated within a system determined by resource issues. The Introduction to this book argued that financial assessment was central to the origins of hospital social work. This task is again becoming a key focus. While older people's state pensions have been subject to substantial reduction if they stayed in hospital for periods of six weeks, and residential care has been means-tested since 1948, the new powers given to local authorities by the NHS and Community Care Act 1990 extended the arena of means testing and assessment and located it firmly within social services. Hospital social workers could not escape the expectations of their managers that they would carry out financial assessments if community or residential services were to be set in place; they were also perceived to be the only people in the hospital who possessed knowledge and expertise about such matters. The hospital based care manager working with Mrs Adams displayed her growing confidence in her own changed role:

I'd never even tried to understand DSS benefits before, but now it's essential and I work well with the DSS

It took me ages to feel comfortable talking about money, I just don't like it – it's as if I'm a DSS Officer and I never saw myself in that role. This is not to say I'm unrealistic – this is the way it is and resources are scarce.

When working with Mrs Adams this care manager was conscious that it was important not to over load her with financial information as she was unwell.

Some care managers linked the emphasis on charging with the need to relate to the commercial sector. One hospital based care manager reflected on the new map of social care: 'Everything has changed for me. In former times I wouldn't think to ask about private residential homes what they were charging, it was left to the relatives to sort. Now I don't think twice about it.'

Hospital based practitioners in Rachman's (1997) study also regretted the redrawing of activities. Others could see the benefit for service users despite their personal ambivalence about working with the commercial sector of care. This 'professional dissonance' (p.221) related to a perceived change in culture but was not solely confined to the hospital or health – social care interface. It appeared to be linked to uncertainty about social work's legitimate place in the world of care management (Bradley and Manthorpe, 1997).

Making and responding to change
We explore here the conflicting pressures to carry out proper assessment of need when individuals' circumstances and wishes are unclear and/or changing. This appeared to be particularly relevant to hospital social work as patients may be confused temporarily after surgery or treatment or disorientated by the move from familiar surroundings and changes in routine, diet or medication. The case of Mrs Walker (previously mentioned on page 77) illustrates this.

At the first assessment interview with the care manager, Mrs Walker, lying in bed, had insisted that she be discharged to the residential home where her husband had recently died. These wishes were accepted by the care manager and became the central focus of the care plan, as discussed above. Three days after this interview Mrs Walker suffered a stroke and from this point her medical condition became increasingly unstable and it proved difficult to conclude the assessment. Initially, the ward staff said that although Mrs Walker needed assistance with personal care tasks, mobility and transferring, this was likely to be a temporary state. By day ten it was clear to the care manager that Mrs Walker was not making rapid progress since she was receiving intensive nursing care. Three weeks later Mrs Walker was slightly improved but was still very poorly. The care manager asked the ward staff to contact her when Mrs Walker was more stable and when it might be possible to update the original assessment. During her sixth week in hospital, Mrs Walker was able to confirm to the satisfaction of the care manager that she still wished to move into residential accommodation. Just a few days later, however, Mrs Walker's health had deteriorated again and the care manager said she was uncertain whether she now fitted the criteria for a residential home or would require nursing home care, but reflected that as it was her expressed wish to move to a particular home she would be likely to settle there. At an allocation meeting during this period, a social services manager went back to the original assessment and questioned whether Mrs Walker was making the right decision or 'just reacting to her grief', but concluded that she was 'better to be in an environment with people around'. The decision to admit her to the home was made, and some two months from the beginning of the assessment Mrs Walker, now slightly better, was discharged to the residential home of her choice.

Pressures on hospital social workers, it appears, do not only emanate from powerful institutions: users themselves remain influential. Such an account also conveys a sense of the changes and indeterminacies surrounding hospital based care management.

The emerging picture
In this study, 71 per cent of respondents agreed or strongly agreed that they were not able to undertake preventative work in their current post. This was only a slightly higher response compared with the community based care managers (67 per cent). Rachman (1997) also identified problems with hospital based workers maintaining a preventative role. In some hospitals their visibility – in ward rounds, social meetings or multidisciplinary team meetings – was reduced because social work managers urged their staff to focus on complex cases.

Both in the hospital and in the community, the care managers in our study felt that they were not able to use discretion in their work. The majority of those working in hospital settings said that they had limited opportunity to use their discretion (65 per cent); similarly their colleagues working in the community agreed (75 per cent), implying that their work was even more circumscribed. Using discretion has been traditionally seen as integral to professional social work. The amount of discretion a professional is able to exercise relates to professional autonomy. However, our study revealed that despite feeling constrained in their work, hospital based care managers experienced high levels of job satisfaction, 94 per cent of them considered that they did a worthwhile job compared to 78 per cent in the community teams. In spite of this high level of job satisfaction, when asked whether they found the current post more or less satisfying than their work prior to the 1993 reforms, almost half of the hospital based care managers were more likely to say that they felt less content (42 per cent). Why was this was the case? Perhaps their former role as a hospital social worker may have allowed them to do more traditional and personally rewarding social work tasks such as counselling and some preventative work. Possibly the pressure was different and the emphasis on charging and related activity was not so apparent. Nonetheless, in spite of this comment, more hospital based care managers saw themselves remaining in their current post during the next five years (47 per cent) compared with colleagues in the field (36 per cent). There may of course be other significant factors which affect career aspirations and career patterns. One hypothesis was that career movement was linked to age profiles and that younger workers would be more inclined to want to change jobs and to develop their careers. However, this theory did not hold since hospital based workers in this study were younger than their community based colleagues. For example, 50 per cent of those working in hospital were aged between 30 and 39 compared with 30 per cent of those working in the community, 22 per cent were aged between 40 and 49 compared with 38 per cent working in the community and finally, 17 per cent were 50 years old or over compared with 18 per cent of community based workers.

Conclusion

Balloch *et al.*, (1999) considered it surprising that there had been so little study of the social services workforce when such research could help assess the impact of change on services and would recognise that staff are central to service delivery. Such studies should incorporate hospital and health related social workers. It is particularly important that their relationships with service users as well as interprofessional working are considered. This chapter has developed a picture of their dynamic relationships with those undergoing assessment for social services.

Much has been said about hospital social workers being torn between health and social services organisations and cultures. Indeed, their origins lie in attempts to address hospital priorities. It is clear, however, that there exist other conflicting demands within their role, many of which are common to all field social workers. These include pressures of time and resources, bureaucratic details versus face-to-face contact and working with relatives as well as users. The future for the care managers we interviewed and their peers seems set to change again with new joint commissioning plans and the rolling out of relationships with primary care groups or trusts. Other relevant policy changes such as the encouragement of rehabilitation emphasised in the White Papers *The New NHS* (DoH, 1998a) and *Modernising Social Services* (DoH, 1998b) may have an impact on their work by involving care managers in new aims or outcomes which stress measurable improvements rather than maintenance or management of increasing debility. To construct such aims social workers will need to liaise with the range of health colleagues in a collaborative sense. Helping to get people out of hospital will probably remain the subtext of their work but it will be important to identify how this movement will be part of a process of recovery or continuing care rather than just a move to benefit wider NHS interest.

Notes
All references to particular service users and care managers in our research have been anonymised. We are grateful to them for their cooperation and to our colleagues Nicky Stanley and Andy Alaszewski for their contribution to this research.

References

Balloch, S, McLean, J and Fisher, M (eds) (1999) *Social Services: working under pressure* Bristol, Policy Press

Bradley, G (1997) 'Translating Research into Practice' *Social Work and Social Sciences Review* 7(1) pp3–21

Bradley, G and Manthorpe, J (1997) *Dilemmas of Financial Assessment* Birmingham, Venture Press

Caldock, K (1996) 'Multi-disciplinary Assessment and Care Management' in Phillips, J and Penhale, B (eds) *Reviewing Care Management for Older People* London, Jessica Kingsley

Caldock, K and Nolan, M (1994) Assessment and community care: are the reforms working? *Generations Review* 4 (40), pp 2–4

Carers National Association (1997) *Still Battling? the Carers Act one year on* London, Carers National Association

Carers National Association/Association of Directors of Social Work/ Association of Directors of Social Services (1997) *In on the Act? social services experience of the first year of the Carers Act* Carers National Association, London

Challis, D, Darton, R, Johnson, L, Stone, M and Traske, K (1995) *Care Management and Health Care of Older People*, Ashgate, Arena

Connor, A and Tibbett, J (1988) *Social Workers and Health Care in Hospitals* Edinburgh, Central Research Unit, HMSO

Davies, M and Connelly, J (1995) 'The social worker's role in the hospital: seen through the eyes of other health care professionals' *Health and Social Care in the Community* 3(5), p301–9

DoH (Department of Health) (1989) *Discharge of Patients from Hospital* HC (89), 7 and LAC (89), 10, HMSO, London

DoH (1997) *Making Partnerships Work in Community Care* Bristol, Policy Press

DoH (1998a) *The New NHS: Modern and Dependable* London, HMSO

DoH (1998b) *Modernising Social Services* London, HMSO

DoH, SSI, SO, SWSG (Department of Health, Social Services Inspectorate, Scottish Office, Social Work Services Group) (1991) *Care Management and Assessment: Practitioners' Guide* London, HMSO

DoH, SSI (Department of Health, Social Services Inspectorate) (1993) *Social Services for Hospital Patients* London, HMSO

Glendinning, C (1998) 'Conclusions: learning from abroad' in Glendinning, C (ed) *Rights and Realities* Bristol, Policy Press

Heaton, J, Arksey, H and Sloper, P (1999) 'Carers' experiences of discharge and continuing care in the community', *Health and Social Care in the Community* 7(2), pp91–99

Howe, A (1997) 'The aged care reform strategy' in Borowski, A, Encel, S and Ozanne, E (eds) *Ageing and Social Policy in Australia* Cambridge, Cambridge University Press

Lewis, J and Glennerster, H (1996) *Implementing the New Community Care*, Buckingham, Open University Press

Lord Chancellor's Department (1999) *Charter for Carers* London, Stationery Office

Manthorpe, J Stanley, N, Bradley, G and Alaszewski, A (1996) 'Working together effectively? Assessing older people for community care services' *Health Care in Later Life* 1 (3), pp143–155

Middleton, L (1997) *The Art of Assessment: Practitioner's Guide* Birmingham, Venture Press

Nolan, M, Grant, G and Keady, J (1996) *Understanding Family Care* Buckingham, Open University Press

O'Sullivan, T (1999) *Decision Making in Social Work* London, Macmillan

Phillips, J (1996) 'The future of social work with older people in a changing world' in Parton, N (ed) *Social Theory, Social Change and Social Work* London, Routledge

Rachman, R (1995) 'Community care: changing the role of hospital social work' *Health and Social Care in the Community* 3, pp163–172

Rachman, R (1997) 'Hospital social work and community care: the practitioners' view' in Auslander, G (ed) *International Perspectives on Social Work in Health Care* Binghamton, NY, Haworth , pp211–222

Scrutton, S (1999) *Counselling Older People* 2nd edn, London, Arnold

Secretaries of State for Health (1989) *Caring for People: Community Care in the Next Decade and Beyond* Cm 849, London, HMSO

Smale, G, Tuson, G, Biehal, N and Marsh, P (1993) *Empowerment, Assessment, Care Management and the Skilled Helper* London, HMSO

Social Services Inspectorate (1999) *Inspection of Social Services Departments' Links with Primary Health Services for Older People* London, Department of Health

Stanley, D, Reed, J and Brown, S (1999) 'Older people, care management and interprofessional practice' *Journal of Interprofessional Care* 13 (3), pp229–239

Stanley, N (1999) 'User–practitioner transactions in the new culture of community care' *British Journal of Social Work* 29 (3), pp417–435

Stanley, N, Manthorpe, J, Bradley, G and Alaszewski, A (1998) 'Researching Community Care Assessments' in Cheetham, J and Kazi, M (eds) *The Working of Social Work* London, Jessica Kingsley, pp69–84

Stevenson, J (1999) 'Comprehensive assessment of older people' *Managing Community Care*, 7 (5), p7–16

Wenger, C (1994) *Support Networks of Older People: a guide to practitioners* Bangor, Centre for Policy Research and Development

Chapter 4
Social Work and Acute Health Care

Bridget Penhale

Introduction

Following the introduction of the NHS and Community Care Act 1990, acute health care services within the NHS underwent a number of major developments, both nationally and locally. More generally there were dramatic shifts in health policy during the last decade (Hunter, 1998). These have been far-reaching in their effect, as have the related developments in relation to social care. The impact of these transformations in the early years of the last decade (the 1990s) look set to continue for the foreseeable future, and have been further promoted by the modernisation agenda of the Labour Government (DoH, 1998a).

This chapter will consider:

- the provision of hospital social work services, in particular accident and emergency services in relation to hospital care and treatment for older people;

- the growing interest in rehabilitation driven by policy statements and the Royal Commission on Long Term Care (1999);

- the provision of social care services for older people leaving hospital;

- many aspects of changes in acute health care provision, including rehabilitation services, although a major focus will be given to accident and emergency (A & E) provision;

- the shift within acute health care provisions towards a primary care led NHS.

Current changes in acute health care provision

This section summarises the principal changes in the provision of acute health services that have been developing on a national level. The past five years have seen a series of shifts within the provision of acute services including:

- increased pre-admission screening of elective patients;

- increased proportion of treatment undertaken on a day case basis;

- shorter lengths of stay for inpatient cases and more rapid discharge from hospital;

- reduction in the number of acute beds;
- increasing intensity of bed usage;
- a political focus on the length of waiting lists for treatment.

As a result there are shorter lengths of stay for hospital inpatients in virtually all medical specialities; the exception to this appears principally to concern provision for older patients (Office for National Statistics, 1998). Those patients receiving periods of inpatient care have been discharged from hospital more quickly than previously, although this has led some commentators to remark that patients are discharged 'quicker and sicker' (Victor, 1992). Lengths of stay in hospital have been reduced as part of the drive towards maximising efficiency within acute hospital services, but also as a consequence of developments and improvements in technologies and procedures. Less invasive forms of intervention are now being used for a number of conditions, for example, treatment for visual problems such as cataracts, which therefore require shorter periods of inpatient treatment.

The development of day case surgery has accelerated, with an increasing number of conditions for which day treatment is now deemed acceptable, such as investigation of gynaecological problems, and with more surgical procedures being performed in day units. The number of day case attendances at hospitals in the UK doubled in the period 1986–1993 (Office for National Statistics, 1998). This rise is due to internal hospital agreements about such matters, and the growth of dedicated units, as well as developments in procedures and techniques. The need for a full admission to hospital for the individual is thus avoided unless some unforeseen event occurs either during or immediately after the procedure. The screening process for elective admission has been developed to include day case surgery. Such screening procedures mean that preparations for treatment or investigation have been speeded up so that once patients have been admitted to hospital their treatment begins virtually immediately.

Nonetheless, a number of acute units have seen bed numbers fall in recent years. Decreases in the amount of inpatient provision are likely to be linked to increases in the amount of day case activity within acute units. Such increases appear likely to continue due to improvements and changes in surgical techniques and available technology. To an extent they offset the reduction in inpatient provision. In addition, the introduction of internal economies within hospital trusts has led to increased competition between adjacent trusts for patients, perhaps leading to some natural wastage of provision, on occasion (Appleby and Harrison, 1999).

The discharge planning process has been assisted by such developments so that planning for early discharge can begin at an earlier stage for patients. This is because shorter stays in hospital require attention to discharge at an earlier stage. The rationale for this is that the relevant individuals who may need to be involved with a patient following discharge can be alerted ahead of time about the likely discharge process. This works, of course, provided that all goes according to the treatment and care plan for a patient and there are no unexpected complications. Discharge planning under such circumstances can thus commence at a slightly earlier stage and may even begin at the point of completion of the pre-admission screening process, which is, of course, not always possible for people who are subject to nonelective admission to hospital, that is, are admitted as emergencies.

Measures of lengths of stay in hospitals in the UK indicate decreases in all medical specialisms over the past five years (see, for example, London Health Economics Consortium, 1996). There are of course likely to be local variations in the extent to which decreases are achieved and maintained. In particular, those specialisms that relate to provision for older people may have longer length-of-stay figures, such as orthopaedics. Some of the local variations may, however, surpass projected national decreases, although again there may well be local differences in the extent to which figures includes the total length of stay in hospital. These may also, for example, include periods of rehabilitation in non-acute hospital provision, so that the length of stay for acute hospitals may in some senses be protected. Indeed, such has been the growth in length of stay that some after-care for operations is now not provided at the NHS hospital site but may be contracted at a hotel. Equally, some NHS care has been contracted to private hospitals. In addition, given that the length of stay is but an average figure, for older patients in particular, this does not give any indication of the number of older people who have very complex needs and who are in hospital for much longer periods of time.

Patients' Charter
The promotion of the Patients' Charter since its introduction by the Conservative Government in 1990 consolidated and accelerated significant changes to hospital care (Klein, 1995). These changes include measures to reduce waiting lists for elective admissions and outpatient care. The Charter sets out clearly defined periods for individuals awaiting hospital treatment, and includes information concerning the individual's right to complain and the processes for exercising this right. National expectations concerning waiting times for first appointments, outpatient appointments and for surgery have also been clearly delineated within charters. This is one area where regular audit

and the introduction of performance indicators based on the charter standards have an impact at local levels.

In conjunction with such developments there also seems to have been a marked increase in public expectations of health care provision. This has been developing throughout the latter part of this century and was probably initiated by the creation of the NHS in 1946. This increase in expectation has been mirrored within Social Services Departments following the implementation of the NHS and Community Care Act 1990 (DoH, 1994). The changes in both health and social care engendered by this piece of legislation seem to have resulted generally in raised public expectations and an increased demand for the provision of care (Harding and Beresford, 1996).

The primary care led NHS

In October 1995, the Secretary of State for Health launched a debate on the future of primary health care. Aspects such as the introduction of new technologies, different ways of working (including fundholding) and changing patterns of care had been part of a series of changes. Following a consultation exercise (National Health Service Executive, 1996), the following principles concerning primary care were developed.

Primary health care should:

- be comprehensive
- provide continuity of care
- be properly coordinated so that it is effectively delivered
- be the gatekeeper to secondary (hospital) care
- address the health needs of local communities as well as those of individuals.

Offering care close to the person's home has to be reconciled with the requirement of clinical effectiveness. The setting for this care is often the GP practice, although the focus is generally on the primary health care team rather than solely the GP. The provision of such care offers better value for money than secondary care, but other indicators of quality include: accessibility; equity of provision (via continuity of care); greater responsiveness to individual and local needs; improved efficiency and effectiveness of care and quality. Not surprisingly, social services departments (SSDs) were perceived by DoH centrally as being important and essential players in the provision of primary care (National Health Service Executive, 1996). An agenda for action was developed as a result of this consultation exercise. This identified the priorities for action and how resources could best be deployed to reflect the needs of different localities within regions. The introduction of health action zones and health improvement programmes in certain areas of the country and, more generally, of primary care groups and the cessation of GP fundholding during 1998 were the result of this initiative (see Arora, Davies and Thompson, 1999, for discussion regarding health improvement programmes).

The main thrust of such changes appears to be the move away from secondary and tertiary (specialist) forms of hospital care towards increased provision to patients in their local communities. Nonetheless, the provision of acute hospital care obviously forms an important part of secondary health care. While more care is being provided at a community level with routine pre-admission screening for elective admissions and post-discharge check-ups being conducted locally at health centres, the hospital is still a central focus. Similarly, while there is an increasing range of treatments including minor surgical techniques being performed by GPs at the local primary care level, these are somewhat limited in scope.

Other developments include improved links between GPs and hospitals through improved communication technologies, so that for example, test results and X-rays are available more rapidly to doctors. The continued development of 24-hour cover services by GP cooperatives to offer improved coverage for local populations and shorter stays in hospital similarly support the development of after-care provided by the primary care team following discharge from hospital. Locality profiles and analyses of health needs by health authorities in recent years should assist further in developing primary care services.

Intermediate services
The development of intermediate services follows the trend noted above towards more community based forms of care. These are generally conceived as those forms of care that fall outside the provision of either acute hospital care or the core of service provision found within general practice. Both inter-mediate settings and intermediate services may be referred to in this context. Two main types of care are generally involved. These are, firstly, short periods of treatment for individuals who do not require general or acute hospital services (for example, short-term admission to community hospital or intensive community nursing). Secondly, there is medium or longer-term care for people with more complex care needs than can be effectively managed within GP services. This includes rehabilitation services but also covers the need for multiagency, multiprofessional responses to provision of care. An example of this is seen in the provision of palliative care services to individuals in their own homes.

A number of health authorities have been involved in recent initiatives concerning intermediate services which have then informed local planning processes. These include such aspects as the exploration of public views about intermediate care; a stock-take of models of community hospital provision within regions and health economic evaluations of the relative costs of different models of intermediate care.

Intermediate settings include provision such as community hospitals; 'hospital at home' services; GP beds; respite or convalescent schemes. It is possible that such services as those providing for minor injuries and certain outpatient clinics; weekend GP clinics; therapy services and an increased amount of day hospital provision will in future be based in community hospital provision where this continues to exist. Alternatively, some local health centres/surgeries or even nursing homes might develop extended roles in future. Social services departments are generally viewed as essential partners within such developments, either in terms of providing staff or facilities or setting such resources in the context of their own planned provision. Equally rehabilitation services may also be developed on more local bases in future as part of the range of continuing care provision (Robinson, 1998). Malin examines this further in the final section of this book. In intermediate provision, as with primary care, a key aim is to provide care and decisions about treatment as close to the person's home as is possible and wherever practical to ensure that diagnosis and treatment decisions occur without delay.

Non elective and emergency admissions

The past five years have seen an unprecedented rise in emergency and nonelective admissions to acute hospitals, which represents a countervailing trend to those outlined above, such as shorter inpatient stays in hospital generally. The national trend appears to be in the order of a compound annual increase of 9 per cent in such admissions, although obviously there are variations within regions and localities (McGlennon and Noble-Partridge, 1994, cited in National Health Service, Anglia and Oxford, 1995). From more local perspectives, the national rise in nonelective admissions has placed considerable pressure on local hospitals. The continued increase in such admissions for acute hospitals is likely to have the most immediate impact on accident and emergency departments and any other admissions units, but all areas of an acute hospital are affected. The majority of these nonelective admissions are of older people; a minimum stay of at least five days would appear to be the norm for such patients once admitted to hospital. A number of health authorities have been consistent in their claims that more could perhaps be done to prevent such admissions (National Health Service, Anglia and Oxford, 1995).

Successive governments have insisted that the NHS must manage the situation more effectively. Given this clear direction, health authorities have conducted a number of projects concerning this area of work since 1994. At local levels, initiatives such as day conferences have been convened, to provide examples of local health authorities working jointly with social services to develop clear and effective models for the provision of emergency care in local areas. These have included all aspects of emergency care and the provision of assistance to individuals in crisis in the community and have not solely focused on hospital based emergency care. Developing more appropriate strategies to prevent admission to hospital has been a political imperative.

Why have hospital admissions risen? Are people sicker, or is the NHS less efficient? A number of different factors appear to be involved in such increases. These include:

- Changing patterns of GP cover 'out of hours' (beyond normal health centre hours): more coverage by locum GPs or 'GP collective' arrangements may mean that an admission to hospital is more likely for an individual. The replacement GP may not be familiar with the person's condition or needs or not know of local services that might be available to support a person remaining at home.

- Less risk-taking by GPs because of concern about possible litigation, which may result in a tendency to opt for an admission rather than treatment in the community. This may be particularly likely if, as noted, the individual is not really known to the GP.

- Inability of individuals, families and GPs to access sufficient health and social care outside of normal working hours (for example, night sitting), which may lead to increased likelihood of admission for some individuals.

- A perception of hospital as a safe place in which to accommodate frail older people in need of care, coupled with an inability to access sufficient community and social care services to maintain people at home at a specific point in time.

- More people with chronic or fluctuating health conditions living longer in the community. The implementation of the community care reforms has resulted in fewer admissions to long-term residential care with more people remaining at home for longer periods prior to any admission to care. It is likely that there will be considerable variation in admission rates between localities. It is also difficult to predict accurately the need for admission and to plan services adequately, particularly at times of marked seasonal variation, for example, during the winter months.

- Older people living at home on their own without adequate support networks which may mean that the likelihood of people being looked after adequately at home is reduced. Indeed the majority of unplanned and emergency admissions to acute hospitals concern older people (Christy and Packer, 1995).

- Individuals living in nursing homes (rather than long-stay, continuing care hospital wards) who may be admitted to hospital for acute health problems earlier than previously. While a continuing care ward, traditionally, would manage acute episodes of illness, a nursing home may be less willing to do so, particularly if access to GPs locally by the nursing home is limited. The result may well be an unplanned admission to hospital.

- Higher public expectations that hospital treatment is necessary and legitimate, for example, that cataract operations are effective and worth some discomfort and inconvenience.

- Raised public expectations for hospital care may result in increased pressure for hospital admission rather than staying at home, particularly if support networks for an individual are limited (Chappell, 1995).

There is no certainty as to which factor, if any, is of critical importance in maintaining such continued and sustained rises in the number of emergency admissions to hospital. Within any particular locality, however, it would seem likely that there is an interplay of several different factors rather than one central factor and that the impact of a particular factor may well vary over time. Continuing concern has been expressed in relation to this phenomenon and the apparent inability of hospital trusts generally to accommodate the extra numbers of people involved. Recent years have seen increased media coverage of individuals being treated and kept in A & E departments for many hours, due to bed shortages within hospital wards (Wardrope, Kidner and Edhouse, 1995). For some people in need of inpatient admission and treatment this has even extended to overnight stays in corridors. Such media coverage, perhaps not surprisingly, has been extensive. This is particularly the case during winter periods of inclement weather.

Following the introduction of the Labour administration in 1997, monies were made available to certain health trusts and social services departments (on a competitive tender basis) in an attempt to deal with and resolve 'winter pressures' on bed availability. The money provided has generally been used to develop innovative schemes, often jointly run by health and social care services within a locality, in order to try and prevent admission to hospital (Millennium Executive Team, 1999). The introduction, for example, of 'rapid response home care teams' to enable individuals to return home with enhanced home care assistance and funded by 'winter pressures' finance has also led to a shift in provision, in particular, for older people. This will be referred to later in this chapter.

The domino effect
This section considers the implications of the changes outlined above for social services. It explores the effects on social care provision, on health related social work provision, and on future hospital social work provision.

Social care provision
Given that one of the main emphases of changes in acute health care provision is a shift towards community based care and away from acute hospital care, it is likely that more social care provision will be necessary in order to maintain people at home. This is in line with existing trends in terms of general community care provision with increased public expectation and demand for social care services. If individuals are either not admitted to acute hospitals but are treated locally, or treated and then discharged from acute hospitals more rapidly, the demand for locally responsive social care services is likely to continue to rise.

Additionally, the potential role of the primary health care team in terms of prevention of emergency admission to hospital has yet to be fully realised. There is a perception that the provision of a more developed and more effective 'out of hours' service from the social services department might well assist in this regard (DoH, 1999c). Alternatively, the development of locally based community networks and resources accessible to local doctors and other members of the primary health care team and primary care groups to provide an emergency service might obviate or delay the onset of a crisis admission to hospital. An example of this could be the development of a night sitting service specific to a local area, or even a 'hospital at home' scheme. However, the commissioning and funding of such initiatives will need to be on a joint social services, health and other agency basis in order to be fully effective and efficient. High levels of collaboration will also be necessary between the agencies involved in order for this type of scheme to be successful.

The development of locally based pre-admission screening and post-discharge check-ups, together with shorter waiting times for surgical procedures, particularly those relating to orthopaedics, will probably have different effects on the provision of care. Here, there is likely to be some increase in the need for short-term loans of equipment, or advice about the same, and short-term services to individuals to assist either prior to surgery or equally during the recovery phase. This may counterbalance the need for longer-term provision of equipment and ongoing assistance to people with more chronic conditions who either previously waited for surgery for much longer periods or for whom surgery was not relevant. Targeting services on short-term cases may diminish overall levels of provision if resources are not augmented. Alternatively, service users themselves may be asked to pay more for services or specific items, such as assistance with bathing or the purchase of appliances.

The potential development of community based occupational therapy services to provide a unified service has been identified as a likely improvement in terms of community provision (National Health Service Executive, 1996). This type of provision would most appropriately be based in a primary care group setting. In such settings, there could be increased self-assessment for and access to small or minor pieces of equipment by individuals. The sorts of equipment that could be covered by such schemes might include commodes, high-level toilets and even basic walking aids. Those working on the increased development of the primary care team to provide more community based care also need to consider the potential role of the social worker within this type of setting; this point is discussed later.

Clearly a unified approach to planning and service development is also relevant here. The need for health and social services to collaborate more fully and effectively than previously, particularly in terms of strategic planning, has been regularly emphasised (for instance, see Hirst, 1997). Concern about the potential efficacy of joint commissioning of services without concomitant joint budgets has also been expressed (Hudson, 1997). In the late 1990s a number of pilot schemes concerning joint commissioning were set up throughout the country (see, for example, the work undertaken by the King's Fund in Knowsley concerning the involvement of older people in community based service provision, Blunden, 1998). The emphasis subsequently shifted in 1998 to the development of health action zones and health improvement programmes in different areas.

Health-related social work provision
The shift towards primary care affects social services provision within the primary care setting, especially given the clearly stated view from the Department of Health that social services departments should be more involved in the provision of primary care (DoH, 1999a; 1999b).

Traditionally, as Lymbery and Millward outline in Chapter 1, there have been a number of models of social work provision to GP practices including attachment and liaison services. These have worked well, given certain situations and circumstances, to the benefit of clients, health and social services staff. Social work liaison schemes with GP practices have been more abundant, although the impression gained is that these have decreased in number since April 1993 because of the increase in workload for district based social workers in adult care since that time. An additional area of slight difficulty has arisen within such schemes when there is a specialism base for social workers. In any case, many GP practices would possibly prefer a generic social work link, rather than a specialist only able to deal with a proportion of the referrals that practices might wish to make to social services.

Given the shift towards a smaller number of primary care group clusters, the notion of attachment schemes is increasingly attractive. This could have particular merit if the attached social workers have a specialism base in work with older people as the majority of referrals from GPs from most localities to the SSD generally concern older people.

An alternative model may be developed in more rural SSDs, where social workers are viewed as an increasingly specialist and expensive resource, which cannot legitimately be expended in the majority of situations that arise within primary health care settings. In this model, referral and reception team workers link with a particular health centre and run sessions based there once or twice a week. Callers are seen on an appointment basis (generally arranged by the health centre receptionist) or on a 'drop-in' basis. Referrals from the primary health care team are screened and filtered by the practitioner and only those referrals meriting a fuller response are taken back to district office for allocation to a social worker or occupational therapist for an assessment. This could be of particular benefit in rural areas, as seen in a scheme established by Norfolk Social Services. The development of such a model demonstrates an innovative attempt to link more effectively with primary care, and is likely to provide earlier assistance to individuals in need.

A more radical model concerns the development of local community based support networks, accessible by the primary health care team at times of crisis, which might equally assist in preventing unnecessary admission to acute hospital care. It is possible that community trusts might be involved in the provision of both health and social care in future on a locality basis, and indeed in some areas of the country, such as Norfolk, this is already occurring. The provision of social work within localities and linked to primary care groups is seen as very much a necessity and an additional resource to be utilised and accessed by all (DoH, 1999b). Provision of an effective 'out-of-hours' service by SSDs is often viewed as critical to these types of development. Further consideration of this potential may be of merit to SSDs, as much of the existing out-of-hours provision appears to fail to meet demand. One of the reasons, apart from issues of resourcing, may be that such 'standby' or 'out-of-hours services' are premised on the basis of providing a 'quick fix' to hold situations until district social services offices reopen (DoH, 1999c). This may be rather than providing assistance that could avert a full-blown crisis from developing.

Hospital social work provision
The provision of social work services to hospital patients is based on an esteemed and lengthy historical tradition as described in the introduction to this book. The origins of modern-day social work are firmly rooted in the tradition of social work within hospital settings (Baraclough, *et al.*, 1996; Platt, 1995). Other chapters in this volume have considered the impact of this historical tradition (see Chapters 2 and 3). What is notable, however, is that while social workers have been based in hospital settings for over a century, their particular contributions, especially in relation to the wider profession of social work, have never been fully recognised.

Moreover, the full range of hospital social work services has not been subject to any national review by the Social Services Inspectorate for some years, although some attention has been paid to discharge from hospital (DoH, 1995; 1998b). The focus on discharge appears to have resulted from a perceived increase in provision of this type of social work in certain areas since the implementation of the NHS and Community Care Act, 1990. This largely followed the emphasis promoted by government on the need for agreements between health and social services concerning discharge planning and joint involvement in assessment for nursing home provision where public funding was necessary (DoH, 1992b). Other aspects of hospital social work provision remain relatively uncharted.

In view of the changes outlined above, a number of models of provision are possible. A minimalist approach would suggest little or no change to existing provision. This would support the adoption of a strategy that relied on the further clarification of future developments in health care provision before determining the direction and scale of change in hospital social work. At the opposite end of the spectrum is a view that sees the provision of social work within a hospital setting as redundant. Additionally, given the renewed emphasis on locality or community based care, with a likely increase in demand within communities, hospital social workers would be better deployed within district offices, and from this base provide a social work service to remaining hospitals.

In between these two extremes there are a number of possible alternatives. The first of these is as follows. If the number of beds in acute hospitals decreases and the number of day case procedures increases, there is likely to be less demand for social work in acute hospitals. This is due to the vast majority of day case patients not requiring either formal social care provision or an assessment by a social worker prior to discharge. Nurses could effectively screen patients and refer on, as appropriate. There may well be a need for a residual number of hospital social workers within such settings, but these individuals would be better targeted on particular and distinctive areas of hospitals.

Such social workers are likely to be more involved with those sections of the hospital with a high number of older patients with needs for assistance in achieving a safe and early discharge home. Those patients with complex needs – for example neurology, HIV/AIDS, traumatic injury, intensive care, oncology and other life threatening conditions – and those using A & E provision would also be included. The provision of social work to some of the above areas, for example, oncology, intensive care or conditions such as motor neurone disease or multiple sclerosis, might be provided through joint financing agreements with charities. These could include, for example, the Macmillan/Malcolm Sargeant Fund; Chest, Stroke and Heart Association; Motor Neurone Disease or Multiple Sclerosis Societies. This is because what is likely to be required is a more traditional hospital social work service, including the provision of counselling, rather than a primary focus on discharge planning. Such liaisons have worked successfully in different areas of the country, with charities funding at least a proportion if not the whole of similar specialist hospital social work posts in recent years. Examples of this type can be found in the Macmillan funded posts at Alder Hey Hospital in Liverpool and elsewhere.

A further set of options for the future of this type of social work provision concerns the development of intermediate services. One possible development revolves around the provision of rehabilitation services at a more local level. This could include both medium-term rehabilitation for older patients (recovering from strokes and so forth) but also longer-term provision for younger severely disabled adults (who have progressive illnesses or head injuries, for example). It is possible that the latter group might be adequately served by appropriate links with care managers specialised in work in physical disability who are based in the community or district. The development of rehabilitation services within community settings could be consistent with district based care managers providing continuity of provision for many disabled adults but linking with a hospital social worker specialising in this type of work.

As far as older people undergoing rehabilitation are concerned, it is arguable that their distinctive and often highly complex and changing needs cannot be met as adequately by social workers from a district office base. If older people are to be transferred at an early stage from acute settings to intermediate centres for further recovery and/or rehabilitation, key aspects of the multidisciplinary teamwork and discharge planning will take place in that intermediate setting. A high proportion of people transferred to such settings will have complex and intensive needs for assistance and for assessment and care planning by a social worker. Provision of social work from a district office setting is therefore less likely to be successful in such instances unless the practitioner is able to demonstrate sufficient commitment and maintain continuity throughout the individual's hospital stay, no matter how long.

Despite the increased focus on rehabilitation it is still evident that community based care managers and their managers tend to regard hospitals as 'safe havens'. It is, however, naive to assume that they fail to appreciate the exigencies of time pressures within many hospital settings, especially those deemed to be acute in service provision. Although time pressures are perhaps likely to hold less immediacy in intermediate settings, care managers can find it difficult to maintain continuity with other professionals. This relates particularly to the need for frequent and ongoing communication within multidisciplinary settings, as outlined in chapter 3.

Although there might be some continuity of contact and service delivery from district bases, various studies have indicated that on-site social workers in hospitals are much more effective than those visiting from a district base outside the hospital (Connor and Tibbitt, 1988; DoH, 1992a). Additionally, the existence of hospital based social work staff specialising in work with older people who participate fully in the work of the multidisciplinary team is likely to prove helpful to older patients and their relatives. Indeed this was the finding of a Social Services Inspectorate study of hospital social work provision prior to the implementation of community care (DoH, 1993).

Nonetheless, a small number of social services departments, mostly those in the London area, have reduced or withdrawn their hospital social workers to be district based in the past three years. From discussions with the Social Services Inspectorate it appears, however, that the majority of local authorities still have hospital based social workers and that many have increased the numbers of social workers in hospitals since 1993 (DoH, 1998c). The role of the hospital social worker has altered, however, to reflect the shift towards increased involvement in discharge planning, in particular with regard to older people. This finding has also been reflected in studies such as those conducted by Davies and Connolly (1995), Rachman (1995) and others discussed in chapter two.

Siting the assessment task of care management in community or intermediate centre may lead to a perception within the acute hospital setting that social work provision is only accessible in these locations. In this type of situation, it could be envisaged that the majority of patients would be automatically transferred out of the acute hospital almost regardless of need in order to obtain an assessment for community care services. The existence of a core of social workers in the acute setting helps to safeguard against this potential hazard. The role of social workers in such instances might be more focused on either specialist provision or speedy discharge planning for those people able to return home from hospital fairly rapidly with a modicum of assistance. Social work provision in accident and emergency settings would also be included within this.

The alternative is for there to be more specific links between social workers at district social services level. If, for example, the community hospital provision alters to be far more locality and district based, as suggested above, rather than specialism based, then the hospital social worker as an outposted member of a district social services team could be a highly appropriate development. Work would then be more focused on individuals from a particular area who were being treated in that locality. This would also be appropriate if it was the case that the majority of those individuals would be returning to live at home. It ties in of course with the increased focus on primary care groups and trusts.

Additional provision of social services personnel to accident and emergency and admissions units might prove beneficial in terms of assisting with the prevention of unnecessary admissions to hospital. Such provision may require round-the-clock presence or availability, beyond normal social work office hours. Alternatively, access by hospital staff to an improved 'out of hours' or crisis service, or even for that service, or a part of it, to be based in an A & E setting may be necessary.

There has been little previous research concerning the provision of social work support to accident and emergency settings in acute hospitals (Lewis, McNabb and Rahman, 1994). The results of a small-scale qualitative study, undertaken in one acute hospital trust in the East of England, are reported below.

Social work in accident and emergency settings: the study
Given the paucity of attention paid to the provision of social work to accident and emergency settings of acute hospitals, a small-scale qualitative study was undertaken in one acute hospital trust during 1998–9. The aim of the study was to explore some of the dimensions of the social work provision within accident and emergency settings, by finding out what health and social work practitioners considered to be essential components of the provision of social work to such settings.

The hospital trust in which the study took place was broadly representative of acute hospital provision. The main area of study was in an acute hospital, previously a district general hospital, covering a large area including urban and rural settings. A small number of interviews also took place in a satellite hospital some twenty miles from the main site. This hospital was also part of the acute hospital trust and included a small A & E department, which was largely in use as a centre for the local treatment of minor injuries. The initial stages of the study included discussions with the chief consultant in the accident and emergency department, with the medical director and the operational director of the trust, who had a nursing background. They agreed to the research taking place and permission was also obtained from the Ethics Committee.

The social services department in the area where the study took place was also consulted at the early planning stage of the project. Information about the study was given and discussions took place with the assistant director responsible for adult care and the senior manager responsible for hospital social work provision. Again, social services representatives agreed to the study. The local operational manager from social services was also involved and provided useful and necessary information enabling access to key individuals.

Interviews

Once permissions had been granted, discussion took place between the researcher and relevant operational managers. Local health or social services managers had provided the names of potential participants who were then contacted directly. An explanation of the project, including an information leaflet about the study, and the background to it, were provided. Confidentiality and anonymity were important elements of such negotiations, and assurances were made that any information given by individuals, for example through the use of direct quotations, or mention of their professional backgrounds would not be attributable. Individuals were then given the opportunity to decide whether to participate or not.

A total of 22 health and social care practitioners were contacted. Of these, two individuals with health backgrounds declined to participate following initial discussion. The reason given by both was lack of experience and knowledge of social work provision within the accident and emergency department. The study therefore interviewed 20 health and social care practitioners. The majority of these (14 in all) had health care backgrounds, although six social work practitioners were involved.

Two of the health professionals were doctors; the other 12 were nurses. Together they possessed a range of experience and worked at both junior and senior levels. It was originally intended to include health care practitioners from other professions allied to medicine, for example, occupational and physiotherapy. However, it transpired that due to internal reorganisation within the Trust, none were assigned to A & E as an area of specialism.

The social work practitioners also had a range of experience, knowledge and status levels. Two were hospital social workers with responsibility for provision to an accident and emergency department; one was an out-of-hours social worker and one a hospital social work manager. Additionally one hospital social worker had previous responsibility for social work provision to an A & E department while another hospital social worker had no responsibility nor experience in A & E.

Interviews took place at the convenience of the participants, but all were held during normal working hours and at the usual workplace of the individuals concerned. In the event, a small number of the interviews had to be rearranged due to particularly heavy demands on the A & E department. This was acknowledged as a potential hazard of this type of research at the time of initial contact with potential participants. Given that the interviews took place during the winter period, it was surprising that interviews had to be rearranged on only three occasions.

Interviews were semistructured and, as might be expected, included a mix of closed and open questions. Initial questions covered biographical details concerning individuals and their professional experience. The majority of questions were, however, open, and allowance was made for interviewees to provide any additional comment and information at the final point of the interview. Questions included:

- the individual's knowledge about the provision of social work to the accident and emergency department
- the sorts of situations in which social work provision would be sought within accident and emergency
- whether existing arrangements were satisfactory
- what happened in terms of social work provision to A & E outside of normal hours
- any alternative models of provision.

Interviews took on average 45 minutes to complete, with a range from 25 minutes to an hour in length. Findings were analysed using a combination of descriptive statistics and a thematic content analysis of the more detailed responses in terms of the themes that developed through the individual responses (Strauss, 1968). The themes identified from the analysis were: awareness and knowledge of social work; access to service; types of referral; out of hours and emergency provision; views about provision of social work service and ideas about future provision.

Study findings

The composition of the respondents was as follows. Three-quarters of the participants were female (55 per cent of the health professionals and 66 per cent of the social workers). The average age of the participants was 45.5 years for the health professionals and 44.5 years for the social work professionals. The respective lengths of experience since qualification were 18.5 years and 13.5 years, with a range from 3 years to 36 years for health professionals and 6.5 years to 22 years for social work professionals. This was generally an experienced and knowledgeable group of staff.

Lengths of experience in working in an A & E department were 10.6 years for health professionals and 8.8 years for social work professionals respectively. The range of lengths of experience in working in an A & E department was from 20 months to 18 years for health professionals and from 3.5 years to 20 years for social work professionals.

The majority of the health professionals interviewed were aware of the nature and extent of the existing social work provision to the A & E department and how to access it. The level of knowledge depended to an extent on the level at which the practitioner worked, as several participants indicated that contact with the appropriate social worker was not their role, but that of a more senior member of the staff team. Medical staff were slightly less familiar with the detail of the arrangements but indicated that they knew how to ensure that referrals were made to the social worker if necessary.

Social work practitioners were generally equally conversant with the existing provision. Neither the practitioner from the out-of-hours service, nor the hospital social worker without direct experience of A & E working was familiar with the detail. As might be expected, however, both knew how to access that information if necessary and correctly deduced that the hospital social work team would provide normal provision.

The range of situations identified by participants in which a referral to the social work department might be made from A & E was varied. The majority of health professionals indicated that social workers would be likely to become involved in the following types of situation:

- older people in need of care and/or support
- child protection and some childcare issues
- patients with needs relating to mental health or overdose/self-harm.

The ordering of those situations was as given above. All but one of the health respondents mentioned the potential involvement of the social worker with older people, and all but three, some 78 per cent, referred to child and family issues. The one individual who did not specifically mention older people worked at night and focused on the particular need for social work in situations of child protection and mental health admissions, which perhaps reflected personal experience of social work provision. Nine respondents (64 per cent) referred to problems relating to mental health, overdoses or self-harm as requiring social work intervention. The needs of disabled people and those relating to a somewhat vaguer group of 'social problems' were also mentioned by a minority of respondents as potentially in need of social work intervention. And, as might be expected, responses included the use of examples from individual's own experiences at work:

> *A person with social problems and a smoke damaged house.*

> *If an elderly person lives alone and needs input at home because they are at risk.*

> *An elderly lady with a broken wrist, unable to care for herself or husband.*

Social work respondents also illustrated situations where social work provision might be needed within an A & E setting. These tended to be longer and to cover slightly more examples than those from health professionals. Even the social worker without any formal A & E experience identified four areas of potential need:

> *'. . . older people, . . . social situations, overdoses, homelessness and that kind of thing. . .'.*

Again, the majority of respondents mentioned the areas of work with older people, mental health and childcare/child protection. All respondents mentioned older people as an area of likely need, whilst mental health and issues in relation to childcare were each mentioned by two-thirds of the respondents.

Interestingly, only one respondent viewed such contact as being in relation to potential admission to residential care, the other respondents indicating likely needs in relation to assisting an older person to return home, with support, following a visit to A & E. The social worker directly involved in A & E had personal experience of very few requests in relation to residential placements from that department. Half of respondents stated that referrals might be made in relation to service users with substance abuse or overdose problems.

Health respondents were clear that the existing daytime provision met the needs of the A & E department. All respondents replied affirmatively to this, although a number gave rather more qualified responses, indicating that provision out of hours could be problematic:

> *Social work cover is adequate. During normal hours this is fine, but not always at night.*

> *Arrangements are fine during the day, but night time and out of hours can be more difficult.*

Social work practitioners generally also considered that arrangements were satisfactory, although the out-of-hours social worker and the social worker without direct A & E experience felt unable to answer this question adequately. All three social workers with experience of A & E working referred to work with individuals with identified social care needs in hospital settings, wherever that might be within the hospital. The two existing workers did not view their role in the A & E setting as constituting a large part of their work, both having other responsibilities:

> *My role is not a big role, I deal with people who don't need admission.*

> *My main role is elsewhere, I don't get that involved.*

The questions relating to social work cover out-of-hours elicited a range of responses. All the health respondents were aware that the systems for emergency cover were different and indicated that they knew how to access these. The level of detail given varied between individuals, perhaps reflecting differing levels of responsibility. This was similar to the earlier findings that some staff knew approximately what the system in relation to mainstream social work provision within the hospital was, without knowing the fine detail of how to access a social worker. Some practitioners (including medical staff) do not have to make direct contact with social workers either in the hospital or the out-of-hours team, as this responsibility rests with another member of the team. Views varied about the effectiveness of the out-of-hours service. Over two thirds of respondents mentioned substantial delays in the social work response at night and at weekends:

> *Generally helpful, but there can be long waits for people to come.*

> *There is usually a wait for the social worker to arrive and the response isn't always good enough.*

> *Night-time and out of hours can be very difficult. An older person coming in late on a Friday afternoon can mean trouble*

Social work respondents also knew how to access the out-of-hours service, if necessary. One respondent, who raised the issue of the out-of-hours service being limited in terms of resources, wondered:

> '*maybe there should be more availability for the public after hours*', whilst another social worker admitted: '*often we and they (the referrer) don't really know what we can do*'.

One of the social workers had previous experience of out-of-hours social work and indicated that this type of work was: '*unpredictable, and mostly you can't plan for it.*'

The final formal question related to whether respondents had ever considered alternative models of social work provision to the A & E department. Very few of the health practitioner respondents appeared to have thought about or considered this possibility. For example, one respondent said:

> *I've not really thought about alternatives . . . we don't usually have to wait too long and with the person in the hospital, if they can help they will.*

Another commented:

> *I don't know what an alternative model would be. You can't run the same service at night, it isn't possible.*

Several of the respondents gave the matter some thought during their response to this question:

> *I haven't thought about it, just accepted the way it's been. A named social worker in the hospital out-of-hours would be useful, though.*

Another replied:

> *Someone on call here 24 hours a day probably wouldn't be used enough, but having someone to access, a named person for us to contact is very important.*

A more senior health professional stated:

> *Social services are sometimes difficult to access. It would be good if we could have direct contact with agencies ourselves, not through a third party. This would be a more holistic approach but then we can't always do everything*

This person also then commented:

> *We couldn't manage without the social worker on site here; she's brilliant.*

Social work respondents were also unlikely to have given the matter much, if any, consideration. One respondent commented:

> *No, I've not thought about it. Contacts with A & E staff are professional and we have good relationships. Whilst another said: 'I've not really considered this. We work with what is.'* However, there were several suggestions as follows: '*Maybe a social work presence there [in A & E] during the day is needed*'.

and:

> '*If it is a big department, somebody based there or on first call for duty would be useful.*'

The majority of additional comments in response to the final open question of the interview concerned the definite need for there to be an identified and familiar social worker in the hospital for the A & E department to contact and to work with. This was so from both health and social work respondents. One health respondent described a named person, contactable by the A & E staff thus:

> *We are very lucky here to have someone so willing to help: it's essential.*

Another stated:

> *Social work type problems are usually sorted without too much problem, but that needs somebody here in the hospital, who we know.*

Whilst another commented:

> *We do extremely well with our social worker on site; it puts nurses' minds to rest that she is here.*

Another statement in this vein was:

> *If we can't use the social worker on site we feel lost, and we have diffi-culty keeping track of the situation. I feel there is a more holistic approach if our social worker is involved.*

At least half of the social work respondents made similar comments in response to this question:

> *Doctors and nurses appreciate our response, we work in partnership in the [A & E] department.*

A further respondent stated:

> *There should definitely be an allocated social worker for A & E work.*

Another indicated:

An attached social worker post . . . there is more of a traditional generic social work role in A & E.

Discussion

The results of this small qualitative study suggest that the provision of social work to A & E departments constitutes a necessary part of the social work role in hospitals. For health care professionals in such settings, appropriate access to a social worker who is preferably personally known to that department is highly valued. Hospital based social workers are seen as important in this regard by both health and social work staff. Health professionals knew how to access the social worker and in general terms were aware of the sorts of circumstances in which referrals should be made to the social worker. They were very positive about the provision they received. A social worker on site, who responds when contacted, was seen as beneficial to the work of the whole A & E department, especially in relation to avoiding unnecessary admissions to hospital beds.

The provision of social work out-of-hours was considered rather more problematic. However, many related this to the context in which the particular service operated. Individuals were therefore not as highly critical of the out-of-hours provision as they might have been, but commented on the need for improvements to that range of provision. In connection with this, over three-quarters (78 per cent) of the health respondents emphasised the benefits of a 'Rapid Response Team' of specialist nurses provided through Winter Pressures Finance and based in the main acute hospital (Millennium Executive Team, 1999). This team was available to assist in returning patients home more easily and speedily during the winter months, and was described as particularly valuable in relation to out-of-hours provision and holding situations until the local social services department could conduct assessments.

In general, respondents had not considered alternative forms of provision, most indicating that they were satisfied with what was familiar to them, as long as this worked! A few of the health respondents did make some suggestions about alternative provision, but they were too small in number for any common categories to emerge. One of the more senior health respondents, who was extremely positive about the social work provision, appeared to be advocating a reduction of social workers in the hospital but then made sure that the extent of the existing staff's commitment and enthusiasm about the provision available to the department was recorded in full! Half of the social work respondents made suggestions about alternative forms of provision. These mainly concerned the need for a ward/A & E department base from which an allocated social worker could operate.

A further model of potential provision revolves around the notion of extending the hours of provision, perhaps through a revision of working conditions within hospital settings, to reflect the fact that hospitals are open round the clock. This might provide more adequate access to social services out-of-hours (DoH, 1999c). To resource this, a base for the out-of-hours team, for example, might have to be established within easy reach of the hospital (if not physically within it). Alternatively, a dedicated out-of-hours social worker to cover provision within a number of hospitals could be provided by the out-of-hours service.

The provision of a hospital social work service is likely, in the view of the majority of those interviewed, to continue to be necessary, if not essential. However, some consideration needs to be given to the organisation of such services. This might include some discussion of whether there should be a separate hospital social work specialism, including out-of-hours coverage to hospitals, and in particular to A & E departments. This would therefore necessitate representation of hospital social work at senior managerial levels within social services departments.

Concluding comments
A number of very different models concerning both social care provision in general terms and more specifically health related and hospital social work provision arise in relation to accident and emergency provision. Decisions relating to such options need to be taken by social services departments in partnership with primary care groups and acute hospital trusts. The minimum position would seem to be to adopt a 'do nothing; let's wait and see approach'. The potential danger of this is that SSDs will remain in reactive mode, responding to changes in health care as they occur rather than taking a more proactive stance. An added danger of the former 'wait and see' approach is that SSDs may yet again have to introduce a set of changes in a relatively short space of time, without adequate planning, to respond to changes elsewhere in the system.

The difficulty with instigating change, however, revolves around deciding which changes to make and the levels and degree of uncertainty about whether particular courses of action are advisable in the longer term. Different pilot projects to test out various assumptions, with adequate evaluation of their effectiveness, are likely to be of particular value to assist in the decision-making process concerning which models to develop and which to reject. Further research concerning this area is also necessary. Such research will need to include the views of patients, and in particular older people and their carers within the community.

An approach such as this would inform the process of change and assist in the implementation and management of whatever change was decided upon. It is unlikely that any one model would necessarily be predominant: rather a number of different models could satisfactorily coexist if properly managed. This would strengthen the likelihood of an SSD responding to more locally based needs, although attention would need to be paid to some of the sensitivities surrounding boundary issues. Maximum responsiveness to and flexibility in meeting the needs of individuals on a local basis should be the cornerstones of future provision of social services within health care settings. Clearly, work with health concerning the development and determination of locality profiles including social as well as health care needs should be of benefit to social services departments. Collaboration and joint working have never been more clearly indicated than in the climate following the modernisation agendas for health and social care.

References

Appleby, J and Harrison, A (1999) *Health Care UK 2000: the King's Fund review of health policy* London, King's Fund

Arora, S, Davies, A and Thompson, S (1999) *Developing Health Improvement programmes: lessons from the first year* London, King's Fund

Baraclough, J, Dedman, G, Osborn, H and Willmott, P (1996) *One Hundred Years of Health Related Social Work 1895–1995: Then, Now, Onwards* Birmingham, Venture

Blunden, R (1998) *Terms of Engagement: engaging older people in the development of community services* London, King's Fund

Chappell, A (1995) 'Rising emergency admissions: patients have rising expectations' *British Medical Journal* 310 (6983), pp 867–8

Christy, V and Packer, C (1995) 'Rising emergency admissions: age, distance from hospital and deprivation are influential factors', *British Medical Journal* 301, p 867

Connor, A and Tibbitt, J E (1988) *Social Workers and Health Care in Hospitals* Scottish Office, Social Work Services, HMSO

Davies, M and Connolly, J (1995) 'Hospital social work and discharge planning: an exploratory study in East Anglia' *Health and Social Care in the Community* 3,(6), pp 363–371

DoH (Department of Health) (1990) *NHS and Community Care Act* London, HMSO

DoH (Department of Health) (1992a) *Social Services for Hospital Patients 1: working at the Interface* London, HMSO

DoH (Department of Health) (1992b) *Implementing Caring for People* (CI (92) 30) London, HMSO

DoH (Department of Health) (1993) S*ocial Services for Hospital Patients 3: users and carers perspective* London, HMSO

DoH (Department of Health) (1994) *Inspection of Care Management and Assessment Arrangements in Social Services Departments* October 1993–March 1994: second overview report, London, HMSO

DoH (Department of Health) (1995) *Moving On: national inspection of SSD arrangements for the discharge of older people from hospital to residential or nursing home care* London, HMSO

DoH (Department of Health) (1998a) *Modernising Social Services* London, HMSO

DoH (Department of Health) (1998b) *Getting Better: inspection of hospital discharge (care management) arrangements* London, HMSO

DoH (Department of Health) (1998c) *Health and Personal Social Services Statistics for England* (1998 edition), London, HMSO

DoH (Department of Health) (1999a) *Working in Partnership: joint working between Health and Social Services in Primary Care Groups* London, HMSO

DoH (Department of Health) (1999b) *Of Primary Importance: inspection of social services departments' links with primary health services* London, HMSO

DoH (Department of Health) (1999c) *Open all Hours: inspection of local authority social services emergency out-of-hours arrangements* London, HMSO

Harding, T and Beresford, P (1996) *The Standards we Expect* London, National Institute for Social Work

Hirst, J (1997) 'Health and social care: all together now', *Community Care Supplement*, 1st October, p1.

Hudson, B (1997) 'Caring Sharing', *Community Care Supplement* 1st October, pp2–4.

Hunter, D (1998) 'The new health policy agenda: the challenge facing managers and researchers' *Research, Policy and Planning*, 16, 2, 2-6

Klein, R (1995) *The New Politics of the National Health Service*, 3rd edn, Harlow, Longman

Lewis, B, McNabb, W and Rahman, S (1994) 'The role of the social worker in the accident and emergency department of a district general hospital' *Journal of Accident and Emergency Medicine* 11(1), pp 21–24

London Health Economics Consortium (1996) *Bed Utilisation in Northern Ireland: report of a utilisation review in 11 Trusts in Northern Ireland* London, London Health Economics Consortium

McGlennan, M and Noble-Partridge, P (1994) An Emergency Review, Stage 1: Data Analysis, Ipswich: Suffolk Health Authority in National Health Service (NHS) Anglia and Oxford (1995) *Emergency Care Handbook,* Oxford: Regional Health Authority.

Millennium Executive Team (1999) *Winter Planning Conference Proceedings* London, HMSO

National Health Service (NHS) Anglia and Oxford (1995) *Emergency Care Handbook* Oxford, Regional Health Authority

National Health Service Executive (NHSE) (1996) *Primary Care: the future* London, HMSO

Office for National Statistics (1998) *Social Trends* 28, London, Office for National Statistics (HMSO)

Platt, D (1995) *The Centenary of Health Related Social Work: a public lecture* Birmingham, Venture

Rachman, R (1995) 'Community Care: changing the role of hospital social work' *Health and Social Care in the Community* 3(3), pp163–72

Robinson, J (1998) *Investing in Rehabilitation* London, King's Fund

Strauss, A (1968) *The Discovery of Grounded Theory: strategies for qualitative research* London, Weidenfield and Nicholson

Sutherland, S (1999) *With Respect to Old Age: report of the Royal Commission on Long Term Care* London, HMSO

Victor, C (1992) 'From pillow to post' *Health Service Journal*,102 (5315), pp 20–22

Wardrope, J, Kidner, N and Edhouse, J (1995) 'Rising Emergency Admissions: bed crises are occurring almost daily in some hospitals' *British Medical Journal* 310 (6983), p867

Chapter 5
From Continuous to Continuing Long-term Care

Vanessa Malin

Introduction

In their introduction to this book, the editors, Bradley and Manthorpe, refer to the challenge in health and social welfare represented by the situation of an older person who is seen as occupying a hospital bed unnecessarily. This powerful image can be further developed, as the person in question may well be awaiting funding from the local authority social services department for a place in a nursing home or resisting pressure to sell her home to fund such care. In this section, this image is explored further through a policy study of the development of approaches to the funding of residential continuous, continuing or long term care for older people within the English welfare state. This confusion of terminology reflects developments in the presentation of national policy. From describing such care as 'continuous care' from 1989 (DoH, 1989, p.33), central government adopted the term 'continuing care' (DoH, 1995) then moved to the term scrutinised by a Royal Commission which considered options for 'long-term' care (Sutherland, 1999) and singled this out as legitimate for the long-term care charter (Department of the Environment, Transport and the Regions and DoH, 1999).

This issue became an area of considerable relevance to social services departments overall and social care practitioners in their daily work as the reforms established by the White Paper *Caring for People* (DoH, 1989) settled into place. Subsequently, further guidance on continuing health care responsibilities for the NHS in 1995 (DoH, 1995) raised the dilemma of identifying the boundaries between health and social care, particularly the boundaries in respect of funding responsibilities. Since the introduction of assessment and care management in 1993 and this further guidance (DoH, 1995), numerous street-level social care practitioners have found themselves in discussions and, at times, disputes with health care professionals over such boundary issues. Such discussions often relate to the extent of their respective agency's support for long-term care through interpretation of the application of local eligibility criteria for care packages and funding of those care packages.

Furthermore, given that social and health care professionals may have difficult discussions and decisions to make over respective responsibilities, vulnerable older people considering long-term care may be even more uncertain about the choices they face. These choices relate not only to the acceptability of the provision of care but also how to fund any social care over and above the entitlement given by the local authority and national legislation. Social care practitioners have to deal with these inherent tensions as part of everyday practice where continuing support has to be accepted by a person and his or her family and informal carers. Social services employees also have to deal directly with the financial assessment of the client's ability to pay for social care provision. This is not of direct concern in the daily practice of the health care professional as, within the United Kingdom, health care is predominantly free at the point of delivery. For the social worker employed in the assessment and care management arm of any local social services department, this area of practice thus represents working on a fault line.

This fault is under considerable pressure. With an increasingly ageing population, the problems associated with long-term support for those unable to manage general activities of daily life, through illness, disability or infirmity, become ever more pressing. In addition, a number of questions arise around this particular fault line for practice and practice development including:

- the ethics of charging vulnerable and older people for care in independent sector nursing homes when nursing care is free in their own homes and in NHS hospitals;

- the role of the NHS in providing care that is free at the point of delivery and available solely on need, not on the ability to pay;

- the budgetary constraints leading to tightening of eligibility criteria and, effectively, rationing of care;

- the lack of clarity of policy from central government despite the outcomes of a Royal Commission on long-term Care (Sutherland, 1999).

This chapter, therefore, summarises the history behind policy in 1999, gives an overview of the current position and likely futures before considering the implications for social care practice.

History and context

The roots of the current problems associated with funding long-term residential care lie in the economic crises of the 1970s when local authorities were no longer able to access public investment monies for new beds in their own provision of residential care for disabled and older people (Timmins, 1996, p.416). Local authority social services departments' residential provision was already supplemented by that of voluntary organisations who, 'From around 1979 . . . began to persuade social security offices to meet the fees for their residents' (Timmins, 1996, p.416). What began as a means of supporting the voluntary sector through a funding crisis as a series of 'one off' benefit adjustments became a matter of national policy by 1983. Social security funding became open for the support of both voluntary and private sector residential and nursing home care placements. This public sector financial support was made available on the basis of financial need, not on any assessed care need, and little attention seems to have been paid to the context of a rapidly ageing population. Timmins (1996, pp.416-7) observed that:

> Private and voluntary sector homes were soon to prove the single fastest growth area in public sector spending. Numbers and costs virtually doubled each year, the bill rising from £10 million in 1979 to £500 million by early 1986. In 1979, just 11,000 people were financed in such homes. By 1992, more than a quarter of a million were, and the bill had reached £2.5 billion. Unwittingly, the Conservatives had created a new state-financed, if privately run, industry.

This unwitting growth, alongside serious criticism from the Audit Commission (1986) about the misuse of £6 billion per annum, prompted government action, and a review, led by Roy Griffiths, was set up. Griffiths reported in 1988, having considered a system of community care that was:

> Scattered around health, social security and the Department of the Environment. It took in hospitals and GPs, local authority social services, voluntary organisations, housing and the private sector. It involved many institutions and many more individuals some of whom were providing enormous amounts of care with precious little support. (Timmins, 1996, p.473)

Ultimately, the Griffiths Report (1988) considered three options but favoured those that used the existing infrastructure of the health or local authority rather than establishing any new organisation. Griffiths argued for the organisational role (although not that of sole provider) to be given to the local authority. He held that much of the services were predominantly social care, and that an ethos of support in people's own homes wherever possible meant that institutional models and medical models of care were inappropriate. In addition, the NHS itself had already been under review and radical plans for reorganisation were under discussion. However, the recommendation that the role of coordinating and organising community care should lie with the local authority was not received well by the Government, and the Griffiths Report (1988) was issued for further consultation rather than adopted immediately as government policy.

Eventually, however, the Government adopted many of the principles and ideas proposed by the report and in a subsequent White Paper (DoH, 1989) community care policy for the next ten years and beyond was established. In summary, government policy was to:

- support people in their own homes wherever feasible

- give responsibility for securing social care to the local authority social services department, thus formalising the pre-existing concept of charging for nursing care according to individual means when this is provided in independent sector nursing homes but not when provided in NHS hospitals or by NHS employed nurses in a person's home or in a residential home;

- establish a limit to the budgets available with, in the early years of implementation, transparent arrangements for the monies that would be transferred from the social security budgets, and require-ments for plans to be agreed with local health authorities and voluntary organisations;

- allow local authorities to use the transitional grant monies alongside monies allocated through the standard spending assessment to purchase a range of care that would support people at home and, only where that was not possible, fund residential sector placements;

- introduce an assessment of individual care needs before provision of services in the individual's own home or placement in residential and nursing home;

- increase the role of the independent sector in a mixed economy of care, and move the local authority into an enabling and commissioning role rather than that of provision.

Initially, it was proposed that these changes come into effect at the same time as the development of the purchaser/provider split in the NHS in April 1991 following the enactment of the NHS and Community Care Act in 1990. However, following concerns about the practicalities of implementation, the reforms arising from the new direction of community care policy were not put into place until April 1993. Since that date, the social services department has held the responsibility for the financial arrangements for placements in residen-tial care for those without the means to secure such care themselves. In effect, the local authority social services department replaced and augmented the role of the social security system, but, within two years of the full implementation of the NHS and Community Care Act 1990, the Department of Health (DoH,1995) was forced to issue detailed guidance on continuing care and, in particular, the responsibilities of the NHS.

In part, this is due to the changes in the provision of welfare since the inception of the welfare state. Timmins (1996, pp.501–2) provided an example of his parents' generation where:

> As this generation aged, the NHS operated on them instantly for emergencies and, sometimes after a wait, for other conditions; . . .Their greater longevity carried a price. When they died cleanly and acutely after a brief illness, the NHS looked after them and well. But if they died slowly and forgetfully, as our grandmother did, first capital and then some of the next generation's income vanished in the longer-term care which, during the 1980s, the NHS no longer provided on a sufficient scale to match the growth in the numbers of elderly.

By and large, this shift was hidden for 'the boundaries between means-tested social care and free health care had shifted significantly, though less as a deliberate act of government policy than as a by-product of the incentive systems created' (Timmins, 1996, p.505). Timmins also argued that some health authorities used the availability of social security monies to close long-stay beds from the mid 1980s and overall such long-stay beds decreased by approximately 25 per cent up to 1993. Whilst there was some purchase of independent sector beds by the NHS 'others made no provision at all' (Timmins, 1996, p.506). As the Audit Commission (1997, p.12) highlighted, neither the contraction in the NHS nor the increase in the independent sector was planned, as 'they happened by default as a direct result of the increase in social security payments. They represent major shifts in policy that have never been debated or agreed' (Audit Commission, 1997, p.12). As such, there was no explicit public consideration of the implications of a shift of nursing care into the independent residential care sector and away from the NHS.

In effect, the implications of these unplanned changes were that the burden of the cost of care, particularly nursing care in the residential sector, had shifted. Whilst people without means had access to funds, initially from social security but after 1993 from the local authority social services department, those with moderate assets faced bills for care that many perceived should have been met by the NHS. With the move to local authority social services department, firmly part of the care system, the perceptions of unfairness may have increased, and national charities such as Age Concern started to increase their lobbying for change.

Such perceptions of unfairness can be firmly related to the national rather than solely local policy agenda. Salter (1998, p.175) noted that effectively health and local authorities had been shielded from the growth in the continuing care market because of the funding from the Department of Social Security, but:

> The community care policy introduced in 1993 closed the loophole and
> diverted the demand back once again to the Health and Local Authorities
> – much to their chagrin, as over the previous decade they had grown
> accustomed to the social security subsidy and duly re-allocated their
> elderly care budgets to deal with other, more pressing, matters. (Salter,
> 1998, p.176)

Thus, other patients in the health services or different vulnerable client groups in
the social care sector may have benefited from the previous lack of attention
paid to the long-term care of older people.

The policies introduced in 1993 should have helped reverse this history of inat-
tention to the needs and requirements of older people. However, within 18
months of the formal establishment of assessment and care management of
older people prior to publicly funded placement in the residential care sector, 'a
quarter of all Social Services Departments (SSDs) were reported as having
insufficient money in their STGs to maintain their purchasing patterns to the end
of the financial year' (Salter, 1998, p.176). Salter also argued that this led to
local authorities raising 'the political visibility of the issue' through attempts to
control demand that included raising the issues of health and social care boundaries with the NHS where:

> the reluctance or inability of SSDs to assess elderly hospital patients for
> discharge to community care in a timescale which suited hospitals led to
> the blocking of beds. A survey by the NHSE in March 1995 found that of
> all patients aged 75 and over occupying a hospital bed 20 per cent were
> waiting to be discharged and of these a third were waiting placement in a
> residential or nursing home . . . In the same year a British Medical
> Association (BMA) survey found that 82 per cent of geriatricians reported
> that the new assessment arrangements delayed the discharge of medically
> fit patients, with the average number of extra days thus spent in a bed
> being 17 . . . Bedblocking in turn had a knock-on effect on the ability of
> Trusts to meet their service provision targets: 45 per cent of Health
> Authorities in 1995 gave bedblocking as the reason for the failure of their
> Trusts to deliver their service provision targets. (Salter, 1998, p.176)

Thus, in the first two years of local policy implementation of agreed community
care plans between health and local authorities, 'The inevitable point had been
reached where officers of local agencies became rather more interested in
survival than they were in cooperation' (Salter, 1998, p.176). However:

It is in no one's interest, least of all local authority social services departments, for beds to be blocked in hospital by patients who could be sent home or to alternative accommodation. The knock-on effect of blocked beds does not just concern patients who are waiting for admission to hospital, nor indeed those who no longer need hospital care and are awaiting discharge. The impact on local authority domiciliary services can be quite significant. Patients waiting for crucial hospital care can become more ill and dependent and thus require, in all probability, additional support from local authority organised home care services. Working together therefore becomes a crucially important part of the agendas of both health authorities and trusts and those of local authority social services departments and other services such as housing, welfare rights, and housing benefits sections (Lewis, 1998, p.282)

This emphasis on the need to work together needs to be seen in the context of increasing pressures for service provision and the impact of policy history. Eleven years on from their previous hard-hitting review (Audit Commission, 1986), the Audit Commission found that 'An ageing population is placing increasing demands on the NHS and social services for long-term care. Unplanned changes that occurred during the 1980s have left a legacy that is still posing challenges for those involved' (Audit Commission, 1997, p.5). Furthermore, four years after the implementation of reforms that, in part, were intended to improve the coordination of care, with the establishment of local authority social services as the lead agency for community care, 'The situation is made more complicated by the range of different agencies involved, including the National Health Service (NHS) and local authority social services departments which provide or co-ordinate much of the social care, increasingly with independent sector providers' (Audit Commission, 1997, p.8). This change is illustrated by the Department of Health's (DoH, 1999b, p.95) own figures on how the residential care sector has developed since the implementation of the NHS and Community Care Act 1990 whereby:

- local authority residential places for all client groups decreased by 47 per cent (55,600 places) between 1990–1 to 1997–8;

- voluntary and private residential places for all client groups increased by 49 per cent (107,700 places).

- Residential places for all client groups increased by 15.4 per cent (52,100 places)

However, in terms of older people specifically:

- local authority residential places decreased by 45 per cent (43,600)

- voluntary and private residential places increased by 45 per cent (85,700)

- an overall increase in residential places of 15 per cent (42,100).

Such changes in provision are also reflected in terms of actual expenditure:

> In 1996–97, gross expenditure in England on Personal Social Services was £9.3 billion. Local authorities' expenditure on services for older people and children accounted for nearly three-quarters of this spend. The largest items of expenditure were for residential care (47%) and day care (38%). Within spending on residential care, most was spent on local authority residential and nursing home care provided by the independent sector. Just under half of all expenditure on day care services involved spending on home care and day care centres. (DoH, 1999b, p.95)

The market for the provision of residential long-term care has, therefore, changed considerably during the 1990s. Thus the editors' example of the concern evoked in respect of an older woman in a hospital bed, seemingly inappropriately, cannot just be seen as a single issue relating to the ongoing care of one person, but needs to be considered as part of a wider and more systemic issue of organising and delivering care between and across traditional boundaries.

Challenges for the NHS in respect of continuing care from 1995

Any existing cooperation was further challenged by developments in national guidance on responsibilities of the NHS early in 1995. Following a damning report by the Health Services Commissioner on the discharge of one man from the NHS prior to the reforms of 1993 (Audit Commission, 1997, p.13), health authorities in England were required to establish local policies in agreement with local authorities for the provision of services to support people with ongoing care needs (DoH, 1995). Guidance made it clear that the NHS should make a significant contribution to meeting continuing health care needs through a range of services such as:

- primary care services

- specialist assessment

- rehabilitation and recovery

- palliative health care

- continuing inpatient care under specialist supervision in hospital or nursing homes
- respite health care
- specialist transport.

Eligibility criteria for each area of care were to be developed, and processes for appeal established. Salter considered that this guidance was seriously flawed for 'As political fudges go this document is a masterpiece because it is essentially promulgating criteria about criteria.' Furthermore, 'In effect it is enunciating criteria about organisational arrangements but not dealing with the detail of the criteria which these arrangements should then seek to establish in order to differentiate between health and social care' (Salter, 1998, p.177). Salter then continued to argue, powerfully, that 'Had the Department done so it would have been publicly trapped by the collision between the absolute rights of the health service and the contingent rights of social care, and duly pulped.' As a result, 'By using constructive ambiguity as a management art form, the Department has sought to create the illusion of positive central action whilst re-directing political attention back to the local level where boundary disputes between health and social care agencies will continue to be part and parcel of official life' (p.198).

Despite this 'constructive ambiguity', the implicit message in 1995 was that the NHS had gone too far in moving away from the provision of continuing care. This perception was reaffirmed by the House of Commons Select Committee on Health in 1996 in its review of governmental approaches to long-term care and its funding. This review concluded that the NHS had moved too far away from its responsibilities in the provision of such care, particularly in terms of general rather than specialist nursing care (House of Commons Select Committee on Health, 1996).

Further support for this perception of the NHS shifting responsibilities wholesale for the continuing care of older people to the social care sector was given by the Audit Commission in 1997 which argued that 'In effect, the NHS has increasingly narrowed its role to that of a provider of acute care' (Audit Commission, 1997, p.13). This had resulted in 'the growth of the independent sector to fill the gaps' (p.82) and 'left social services in a position where they have had to follow the NHS rather than set their own priorities and pursue, for example, a more preventative agenda' (p.82). However, the Audit Commission also emphasised that national government policy needed to be developed to address six key questions (see Table 5.1).

Table 5.1   Key policy questions

1	Where should the boundaries of responsibility lie between the NHS, social services, housing and other agencies?
2	What is the role of the NHS in long-term care?
3	Should national standards be set for care, and if so, how should these be implemented, funded and measured?
4	What is the correct balance between acute and preventative and rehabilitative services?
5	Should direct payments be extended to older people to strengthen the user's influence? If so, what does this mean for the role of social services?

Source: Audit Commission, *The Coming of Age: improving care services for older people* London, Audit Commission, 1997, p.82.

Furthermore, in developing answers to such questions, any government review 'might address the issue of how far the state has a responsibility to support individuals, and how far individuals should plan for their own needs' (Audit Commission, 1997, p.83).

This area of policy debate became part of the manifesto commitments for the Labour Party in the preparation for national elections in 1997, and it undertook to establish a Royal Commission to address the issue of long-term care if elected (Prime Minister, 1999). Following a landslide victory in May 1997, the new Labour Government announced the appointment of such a Royal Commission in December 1997, that is:

To examine the short and long-term options for a sustainable system of funding of long-term Care for elderly people, both in their own homes and in other settings, and within 12 months to recommend how, and in what circumstances, the costs of such care should be apportioned between public funds and individuals having regard to:

• the number of people likely to require various kinds of long-term Care both in the present and through the first half of the next century, and their likely income and capital over their lifetime

- the expectations of elderly people for dignity and security in the way in which their long-term Care needs are met, taking account of the need for this to be secured in the most cost-effective manner

- the strengths and weaknesses of current arrangements;

- fair and efficient ways for individuals to make any contributions required of them

- constraints on public funds; and

- earlier work done by other bodies on this issue.

In carrying out its remit, the Royal Commission should also have regard to:

- the deliberations of the Government's comprehensive spending review , including the revision of pensions

- the implications of their recommendations for younger people who by reason of illness or disability have long-term Care needs.

The Commission's recommendations should be costed (Sutherland, 1999, p.ix).

Thus the Royal Commission was clearly tasked to address both funding and care issues, with the underlying message that the Government expected some balance of financial responsibility between the individual and the state. While the Royal Commission did not report until March 1999, in the interim the direction of government policy for health and social care was further established through a series of policy statements (see, for example, DoH, 1997a; DoH, 1998) and guidance (see, for example, DoH, 1997b; DoH, 1997c). The approach to modernisation for the social services was particularly relevant as it set out the philosophical approach underpinning the Government's response to the Royal Commission on long-term Care.

The modernising agenda

By 1998, the Department of Health expressed strong criticisms of social care provision as inherited from the previous government. It observed:

> Decisions about who gets services and who does not are often unclear, and vary from place to place. Eligibility criteria are getting ever tighter and are excluding more and more people who would benefit from help but who do not come into the most dependent categories. Decisions about care can still be service driven, and concentrate on doing things for people according to what is available, rather than tailoring services to the needs of individuals and encouraging those who are helped to do what they can for themselves. (DoH, 1998, section 2.3)

This continuing problem of service-driven care rather than individual-centred services was compounded by a lack of information about services and on financial contributions. In addition, local authorities were seen to be 'tending to focus more and more on those most dependent people living in their community' (DoH, 1998, section 2.6) with the result that:

> although there has been an increase in the overall level of domiciliary care supporting people in their own homes, that increase has been concentrated on those getting more intensive support, and the number of people receiving lower levels of support has actually dropped. . . . This means that some people who would benefit from purposeful interventions at a lower level of service . . . are not receiving any support. This increases the risk that they in turn become more likely to need much more complicated levels of support as their independence is compromised (DoH, 1998, section 2.6)

Pressures on resources since the introduction of assessment and care management for older people in 1993 have led to continued perverse incentives towards responding to dependency rather than preventing deterioration in functioning. As functioning deteriorates, however, there is a further perverse incentive towards placement in the residential or nursing home sector for 'the evidence is that many authorities are setting a financial ceiling on their domiciliary care packages, particularly in services for older people, which can lead to premature admissions to care homes when care at home would have been more suitable' (DoH, 1998, s. 2.7). In addition, this pressure towards placement in the residential sector was further compounded by ongoing rises in the number of emergency admissions to hospital by people over 75 (s. 2.8). Arguably 'These admissions . . . are avoidable in many cases' (s. 2.8.), and increased provision of rehabilitation or recuperation services could help older people return to their own homes rather than to permanent institutionalisation.

One of the reasons that institutionalisation becomes permanent is that 'Once services are being provided, they are often not reviewed. This again contributes to a culture of dependency rather than one of enablement' (DoH, 1998, s.2.9). The government subsequently undertook to ensure that reviews are carried out three months after admission to a care home and then annually (1998, s. 2.19). However, such reviews may not prevent the culture of dependency unless the financing of at least the initial three-month period is addressed, as the individual may be affected by the loss of his or her own home should it be sold to pay for care or where rent cannot be maintained by the tenant due to the transfer of state support from housing benefit to residential care allowance.

In beginning to address these pressures towards permanent residential care being the most common solution for high dependency care for older people, the government made a commitment 'to put greater independence at the heart of social services for adults' (DoH, 1998, s. 2.11). Resulting government action included promotion of independence with special monies in terms of a partnership grant (health and social services) and a prevention grant: together these amounting to approximately £750 million over three years within a modernisation fund of £1.3 billion. Furthermore, the direct payment scheme initiative is being opened to those aged over 65, with other changes being considered as part of a review. Subsequently, the government has made a commitment to increasing the funding for social services 'by an annual average of 3.1 per cent above inflation over the next three years' (DoH, 1998, s. 7.10) This is in addition to increases in standard spending assessments and existing specialist grants and so 'there will be in total nearly £3 billion extra resources for social services over the next three years' (s. 7.12).

The Government subsequently reported on progress in March 1999 (DoH, 1999a). In a more philosophic vein it outlined a series of key objectives for public sector health and social care:

> To enable people who are unable to perform essential activities of daily living, including those with chronic illness, disability or terminal illness to live as full and normal lives as possible. By
>
> * providing care according to individual need regardless of organisational boundaries
>
> * helping people to live independently, and supporting them wherever possible in their own homes
>
> * securing appropriate and effective social care for those who lack the means or other support to get the help they need; and
>
> * giving people who need access to effective palliative care. (DoH, 1999a, p.92)

This, effectively, reinforced the emphasis on overcoming the difficulties of cross-agency and sector working, and continued the policy dimension of support within the individual's own home. However, the differentiation between the availability of social care on a targeted basis and that of health care on a needs-led basis remained. The findings of the Royal Commission on Long-Term Care demonstrated the realities of continuing care for people in 1999.

The Royal Commission on Long-Term Care for the Elderly

Sutherland (1999, p.8) noted that 'About 600,000 people over the age of 65 are getting home care from a local authority. About 480,000 older people are in care homes – that is 1 in 20 of all elderly people.' Such long-term care services cost £11.1bn in 1995 (Sutherland, 1999, p.9) with approximately £7.1bn (64 per cent) coming from the state and £4bn (36per cent) from older people themselves. With £8.3bn (75 per cent) of the total spent in the residential and nursing home sector financial resources are heavily invested away from the domiciliary support sector. However, this is a partial cost analysis for it excludes:

- general practitioner services

- living costs and rent for ordinary or sheltered housing

- social security expenditure.

Furthermore, the figures for contributions from older people themselves need to be viewed in the context of estimates based on 1995–6 data that 44 per cent of single people aged 75 and over in private households had assets of under £16,000 (Sutherland, 1999, p.12). Thus, for the current generation of older people, considerable state support towards the costs of long-term care may be necessary into the future.

But what of the future? The Royal Commission identified a series of factors that will influence the demand for long-term care up to 2050. These include demographical change, health expectancy and the supply of informal care. In terms of the demographical change, Sutherland (1999, p.14) predicted that 'By 2050 the biggest relative increase of older people is expected in the number of those aged 85 and older – 'the oldest old'. They will be three times more numerous in 2050 than now.' The health of this group is seen as 'a key determinant of the need for long-term care' (p.14) with three potential scenarios where, although more people are living longer, they may:

- **experience fewer years of ill health**, the future need for long-term care for each person may reduce and the total may not go up very much from what it is now

- **experience no longer periods of ill health than the current generation** – the need for long-term care for each person will be the same, although the total need will rise

- **experience more ill health for longer**, the need for long-term care will increase both for each individual and in total (Sutherland, 1999, p.14: author's emphases).

Any one of these scenarios may apply but 'The best evidence we can find about the United Kingdom suggests that the factors which are causing us to live longer are also resulting in the extra years of life being free from severe disability' (Sutherland, 1999, p.15). Thus the increasing number of very elderly people may not lead to as high a demand for long-term care as that currently provided for the equivalent population.

However, although the health of older people may improve, predicting the future is further compounded by changes in the provision of informal care, and Sutherland (1999, p.17) argued that 'Whether there will be a reduction in the supply of unpaid care in the future is one of the most difficult questions we have been asked to consider.' The Royal Commission thus assumed that 'there will be no real change in the future availability of informal care' (p.18).

Nonetheless, despite these predictions, the Royal Commission's main report considered that costs of formal long-term care could rise from £11.1bn in 1995 to £45.3bn in 2051 (p.20). These figures should be seen in the context of predicted growth in national income when they represent 1.5 per cent GDP in 1995 and 1.9 per cent GDP in 2051 (Sutherland, 1999, p.20). The question then arises as to how such increases should be financed, and this issue split the Royal Commission in two.

The majority report of the Royal Commission (Sutherland, 1999, pxvii) made two key recommendations:

- The costs of long-term care should be split between living costs, housing costs and personal care. Personal care should be available after assessment, according to need, and paid for from general taxation: the rest should be subject to a co-payment according to means.

- The Government should establish a National Care Commission to monitor trends, including demography and spending, ensure transparency and accountability in the system, represent the interests of consumers, and set national benchmarks, now and in the future.

These two recommendations were based upon three principles: shared responsibility between state and individual, fairness and equity, transparency of resources and responsibility. However, whilst the concept of the National Care Commission gained broader acceptance, a minority report challenged the concept of personal care being the responsibility of the state. Joffe and Lipsey (1999, p.113) argued that such state provision would be affected by the impetus towards improved standards in the residential care sector, and this in turn would be affected by increases in demand for such care simply because it was free at the point of delivery. They were also less accepting of the assumption that less disability and debility would be associated with the increasing very elderly population. To Joffe and Lipsey (1999, p.114) 'First, the state must estimate and cost the minimum standards of care that it believes to be acceptable and then fund these costs. Second, it must decide what is to be funded by the state and what by elderly people themselves.' In summary, Joffe and Lipsky (1999, p.115) make recommendations in respect of funding to:

- modify means-testing so it is less severe and does not impose the need to sell a home

- restrictively define nursing care and make that free in nursing homes which would 'get rid of the worst anomaly in the existing system'

- develop public–private partnerships to fund care including private insurance

- ensure public funding used efficiently and effectively with integrated budgets.

In effect, Joffe and Lipsky argued for incremental changes to the current system rather than the more radial approach of the main report. Clearly, they anticipated that the differentiation between nursing and social care can be made and judged, whereas the majority report, with its emphasis on free personal care, recognised the inherent difficulty that practitioners face in judging where health care begins and social care ends. However, Joffe and Lipsky (1999, p.115) also identified the two underpinning 'schools of thought which have dominated the post-war debate about how long-term care should be provided.' These are respectively described as the 'statist' and the 'free market' philosophy.

The statist philosophy 'dominated 'left' thinking roughly from the end of World War II until the mid-1970s . . . long-term care, like health and social benefits, is the right of every citizen . . . allocated on the basis of need, not wealth, and paid for from taxation' (Joffe and Lipsky, 1999, p.115). However, for many of the current generation of older people, this philosophy underpins their expectation of the Welfare State and thus it should not be surprising that there is considerable disquiet at having to pay for long-term care, particularly where it involves payment for nursing home care. Future generations may be more willing to accept the free market philosophy which came into force from the 1970s and 1980s and 'emphasises individual responsibilities, not rights; the inefficiencies of state provision and the virtues of private provision; and the political and economic limits to taxation' (Joffe and Lipsky, 1999, pp.115). Thus, with all the expert knowledge and predictions available to the Royal Commission, the end result of considerable deliberation is dissent on how to fund formal long-term-care for the next 50 years and beyond and no single set of recommendations for policy makers, pressure groups or older people themselves to adopt.

The policy response
It is hardly surprising, that whilst the Royal Commission reported in March 1999 (Sutherland, 1999), at the time of writing the Government is still considering some of the recommendations – particularly those related to the financing of long-term care through the public sector – whilst introducing a long-term care charter, setting up a National Care Commission, establishing a programme of 'Better Government for Older People' (Prime Minister, 1999, p.78) and preparing a national service framework for older people which 'will set national standards and define service models for older people, put in place programmes for implementation, and establish performance measures against which progress will be measured' (DoH, 1999, p.96).

The House of Commons formally debated the Royal Commission's majority and dissenting reports in December 1999 (House of Commons, 1999). In setting out the grounds for the debate, the Secretary of State for Health claimed that 'A growing elderly population is a success, not a failure; it should be celebrated, not denigrated. Older people are valuable in our society, not a burden on it' (House of Commons, 1999, Column 444). He continued to argue that whilst care standards across the country were variable:

> There are very real concerns about the funding of long-term care. Although only one in five old people need long-term care, as they approach old age many more become anxious about how well they will be looked after, how much it will cost and who will pay. The current system has failed to be explicit about these issues, not least because it has developed in such an ad hoc way in recent decades . . . The current system of care is confused and confusing. It provides too many incentives to care for old people in care homes and too few incentives to care for them in their own homes (House of Commons, 1999, Column 445).

Given that this statement summarised the Secretary of State's view of the existing system of public sector provision and commissioning of long-term care, there was significant challenge from the House of Commons. This challenge was summarised by Leigh (cited in House of Commons, 1999, Column 447) who claimed 'There is a royal commission report, and the

Secretary of State passed over it in about four minutes. It was allowed to gather dust for six months. Is it true that the report will never get out of the long grass because its recommendations will be too expensive?' The Secretary of State for Health subsequently acknowledged that 'Many of the royal commission's suggestions for changes to the funding system for long-term care have substantial costs implications, both now and for the future' (House of Commons, 1999, Column 450), and identified that government proposals on future funding of long-term care would be announced in Summer 2000. He argues that the government:

> shall base any future reforms in this area on three key principles: choice, fairness and quality . . . our policy will be that people should provide for themselves where they are able to do so. In particular, people prefer and should have the opportunity to remain at home for as long as possible. There will, of course, be situations where a person needs to be admitted to a residential care or a nursing home, and that choice should be available, but any reforms to the system of long-term care must reflect and reinforce the crucial policy objective of encouraging independence through choice. We know that we need to find a fairer way of funding long-term care for the future (House of Commons, 1999, Column 450).

The Secretary of State also announced that 6 parameters in respect of funding of long-term care needed further work to ensure that the issues of choice and fairness would be addressed. These can be summarised as follows:

- whether nursing care should be provided free of charge in any setting if a definition of nursing care can be agreed;

- development and design of attractive long-term care insurance and other financial products;

- exploring potential change to residential charging rules;

- transferring income-support residential allowance and preserved rights from the social security benefit system to local authorities;

- further work on guidance on continuing health care;

- reviewing charges for home care and, particularly, the variations in charging policies between local authorities.

In practice, the outcomes of these issues are likely to lead to greater consistency between local authorities and, perhaps, a more consistent approach nationally. This prediction is underpinned by the additional announcement to the House of Commons (1999, Column 448) by the Secretary of State for Health that the Government would:

consult on new guidance to give everyone fairer access to social services. We want to iron out the unacceptable variations that exist at present and to create a fair set of rules and procedures that everyone can follow and understand. The aim will be to achieve greater consistency between local authorities in the way that they apply eligibility criteria for accessing all adult social services, including long-term residential care. Importantly, the guidance will stress the need to align social services criteria with NHS continuing health care criteria. It will also stress the need to agree eligibility criteria with housing agencies to ensure a properly co-ordinated response to people's needs.

In part, this move towards greater consistency has resulted from pressure from groups like Age Concern to reduce what can best be termed a 'postcode lottery' in respect of the provision of public sector health and social care support for people with long-term care needs. However, the announcement in the House of Commons in December 1999 was also affected by case law in respect of relative responsibilities for nursing care.

The legal challenges:
R v North and South Devon Health Authority ex parte Coughlan, 1999
This case law follows a ruling by the Court of Appeal Civil Division (*R v North and East Devon Health Authority ex parte Pamela Coughlan*, 1999) that led to further guidance (DoH, 1999) on the implications for the assessment of need for long-term care and for the funding of such care. In this example, Ms Coughlan – a physically disabled woman – challenged a decision by North and East Devon Health Authority to close her NHS home and place her in a private sector care home outside of NHS care. She was supported in making her case by the Royal College of Nursing who hold the view that 'The simplest, fairest and most cost-effective solution would be to entitle all those assessed as needing long-term nursing care to receive that care free under the NHS, wherever it is provided' (BBC News, 1999). Ultimately, the Court of Appeal ruled that some people would have to pay for nursing home care but that for Ms Coughlan, who had written assurances that the NHS would provide a home for life, should continue to receive NHS care on a non-means-tested basis and available due to need.

The Royal College of Nursing claimed (BBC News, 1999) that 'The judgement clearly states that North and East Devon Health Authority's eligibility criteria for long-term NHS health care were unlawful. It rules that where a patient's primary need for accommodation is a health need, then the patient's nursing care is the responsibility of the NHS and not the local authority.' However, Age Concern argued that the ruling 'perpetuated a fundamental inequality –the fact that people in nursing homes had to pay for care when it is free everywhere else. Nursing care is rightfully a health responsibility and Age Concern has long argued that nursing care should be free at the point of delivery to all those who need it, wherever they live' (BBC News, 1999).

This case thus served to heighten awareness of individual inequity and policy confusion.

It did, however, also explicitly engage the nursing profession in the debate through the professional association of the Royal College of Nursing. Subsequently, a Royal College of Nursing survey is widely reported with headlines such as 'Elderly 'cheated out of free NHS care' ' (Frean, 1999) with commentary that 'Almost 90 per cent of health authorities surveyed by the college were found to be using unlawful criteria to decide if elderly people in residential care were entitled to free nursing care on the NHS' (Frean, 1999). This perception was challenged by the DoH and by the NHS Confederation who 'concedes that some criteria used may be problematic but feels that this report by the Royal College of Nursing lawyers presents a particularly partisan analysis' (NHS Confederation, 1999).

Such 'partisanship' is apparent throughout the policy developments with the conceptual changes from continuing to continuous to long-term care. For individuals facing decisions about care options to cope with debility and disability, the issue is immediate and emotive. For policy makers, the issues relate to both quality of care and affordability of supporting such care from public monies. Social work practitioners have to deal with the consequences of these dilemmas on a day-to-day basis whilst debates continue about the best way forward between the 'leftist' and free market views.

Likely futures?
The potential scenarios for the future cannot simply be constrained to theoretical and policy debates about the quality and financing of residential and nursing home long-term care. There are alternatives for society to consider. Such alternatives include models of more extensive support at home with increased use of modern technologies. There are also issues arising from the growing wealth of individuals and their families with increased home ownership and availability of pension income possibly indicating that the local authority social services department's welfare provision will become more and more limited in its application. Questions arise about the equity of this. Is it fair that only those:

- without the means to support themselves receive an assessment of their needs and advice on the appropriate range of care options?

- with the means to support themselves have to use their own capital and revenue assets for personal care?

For local authority social services departments, there are serious dilemmas arising from both the balance of services to be provided to respond to the needs of local residents and from the disputed nature of health and social care boundaries. The range of such significant government-initiated activity over the past decade indicates that the care of those requiring ongoing support from the public sector is an area of significant policy concern. It should be noted, however, that this policy concern is not solely a matter for the United Kingdom. Saltman and Figueras (1997, p.216) argued that 'the interface between social care and health care remains underdeveloped in many European countries' and continue to suggest that

> Some governments are seeking to redefine health service functions in order to transfer them to the social services, thus separating the 'cure' and 'care' processes. In some cases, the motivation between this type of substitution lies in the fact that, while health services are free of charge, social services are subject to some form of cost sharing, thus becoming a case of substitution of private for public finance. In other areas, social and health care services are pooling resources, particularly in the provision of services for elderly people. (Saltman and Figueras, 1997, p.216)

As a result, Saltman and Figueras proposed that 'The formulation of new options blurs the boundaries between the various aspects of the care system' (p.216). In part this has arisen across Europe as the drive for efficiency in health care has led to pressures on the hospital sector, particularly in the effective use of hospital beds and improvements in securing discharge from the hospital. Saltman and Figueras considered that these European-wide drives towards effectiveness and better discharge 'generally involve shifting costs to individual users or their families' (p.224) either through direct payment or indirectly with dependence on family members for care provision. However:

> The growth in the number of women in the workforce, an increase in the proportion of people living alone, and changing public expectations will make such policies more difficult to introduce, particularly if a 'contract' to provide various types of state support for the elderly or chronically sick has been established by years of payment into some of state insurance scheme. (Saltman and Figueras, 1997, pp.225–6)

In England, the issue of boundaries of responsibility between the NHS and the provision of means-tested social care has not yet been resolved, despite the recommendations of the Royal Commission (Sutherland, 1999). Indeed, when questioned on the definition of such boundaries, Dobson, the then Secretary of State for Health, advised the House of Commons Select Committee on Health (1999, section 33) that 'I do not think there can be a definitive definition, personally, because I think the two things merge into one another.' Dobson was not alone in his difficulty, for nobody else presenting evidence to this select committee could give a definition either. However, in practice, assessing who is responsible for the funding of care means that such boundaries have to be negotiated by the social care practitioner and older people themselves.

Implications for social care authorities and practitioners
As the Audit Commission (1997, p.79) argued 'The pressures to provide good services for older people are likely to continue to grow as the numbers of older people increase over the coming years, and as expectations rise.' Yet the government currently shows no signs of fully implementing the recommendations of the Royal Commission's majority report (Sutherland, 1999). However, recent press reports indicate that 'Those middle-class families hoping to inherit the home of a grandparent or elderly relative are to be thrown a lifeline by the Government, which plans to pay for the nursing of pensioners who live in care homes' (Prescott, 2000, p.1). Prescott identified a senior Whitehall source as saying

> We will make sure that we pay for a daily bed bath by a qualified nurse who can watch for bed sores . . . but we will not be paying for the man who empties your bin or the person who brings you a cup of tea.

Furthermore, 'Government insiders said estimates suggesting that the royal commission's recommendations would cost £1.2 billion were wrong. By paying close attention to which services should be defined as "nursing", the cost to government would in fact fall to about half this.' However, the question of the definition of 'nursing' will, no doubt, engender further debate between health and social care practitioners about boundaries.

In the short term, therefore, it can only be assumed that the local authority social services department and the social work practitioner will continue to have to resolve the dilemmas of long-term care and support for those in financial need. Salter argues that:

> Each fresh negotiation of eligibility criteria redefines the boundary between health and social care and creates a different input to the health service. Each failure to negotiate a settlement means that the problem is formally delegated to the professionals who make the decisions about

assessment and access. Even where eligibility criteria are agreed, they are frequently sufficiently obscure to require interpretation by professionals anyway and thus, given finite resources, act as a focus for inter-professional disputes around control of the rationing function. Consultants, GPs and nurses vie with social workers and care managers for the power to determine which patients should go where and who should pay for them. (Salter, 1998, p.183)

Even though some of the dilemmas associated with the inequitable costing of nursing care may be addressed if the Royal Commission's report is adopted, the difficulties of implementation of eligibility criteria based on potentially disputable definitions of nursing care will remain.

References

Audit Commission (1986) *Making a Reality of Community Care* London, HMSO.

Audit Commission (1997) *The Coming of Age: improving care services for older people* London, Audit Commission Publications.

BBC News (1999) *Health:* 'Coughlan case sparks long-term care debate', *BBC News,* London, 16 July. http://news.bbc.co.uk/hi, viewed 2 December 1999.

Department of the Environment, Transport and the Regions and Department of Health (1999) *Better Care, Higher Standards: a charter for long-term care* London, Department of Health.

DoH (Department of Health) (1989) *Caring for people: community care in the next decade and beyond* London, HMSO.

DoH (1995) HSG(95)8/LAC(95)5: *NHS Responsibilities for Meeting Continuing Health Care Needs* London, Department of Health.

DoH (1997a) *The New NHS: modern, dependable* London, Stationery Office.

DoH (1997b) *Priorities and Planning Guidance* London, Stationery Office.

DoH (1997c) *Better Services for Vulnerable People* EL(97)62, London, Stationery Office.

DoH (1998) *Modernising Social Services* London, Stationery Office.

DoH (1999a) *The Government's Expenditure Plans 1999–2000 – departmental report: the health and personal social services programmes* London, Stationery Office.

DoH (1999b) *Ex parte Coughlan: follow up action. Continuing health care: follow up to the Court of Appeal judgement in the case of R. v. North and East Devon Health Authority* HSC 1999/180 LAC(99)30, London, DoH.

Frean, A (1999) 'Elderly "cheated out of free NHS care" ' *The Times* 2 December p2

Griffiths, R (1988) *Community Care: an agenda for action* London, HMSO

House of Commons (1999) 'Long term care' *Hansard* 2 December. http://www.publications.parliament.uk/

House of Commons Select Committee on Health (1996) *Long Term Care: future provision and funding* Third Report Session 1995-1996, HC 59-1, London, HMSO

House of Commons Select Committee on Health (1999) *The Relationship between Health and Social Services, First Report Session 1998–1999* London, Stationery Office. http://www.parliament.the-stationery-office/

Joffe, J and Lipsey, D (1999) 'Note of dissent' in Sutherland, S (Chairman) *With Respect to Old Age: Long term care –rights and responsibilities* Report of the Royal Commission on Long Term Care London, Stationery Office

Lewis, B (1998) 'Working with local authorities' in Merry, P (ed) *The NHS Confederation: 1998/99 NHS handbook* 13th edn. Tunbridge Wells, JMH

NHS Confederation (1999) 'Huge cost implications if changes are made to long-term care eligibility' December 1st *News Release* http://www.nhsconfed.net/news/ viewed 3 December

Prescott, M (2000) 'Government to pay care home bills for elderly' *Sunday Times* pp1–2, 13February

Prime Minister (1999) *The Government's Annual Report 98/99*, London, Stationery Office

R v North and East Devon Health Authority ex parte Pamela Coughlan (1999)

Salter, B (1998) *The Politics of Change in the Health Service* London, Macmillan

Saltman, R and Figueras, J (1997) *European Health Care Reform: analysis of current strategies* Copenhagen, World Health Organisation Regional Office for Europe

Sutherland, S (Chairman) (1999) *With Respect to Old Age: long-term care – rights and responsibilities* Report of the Royal Commission on Long Term Care, London, The Stationery Office

Timmins, N (1996) *The Five Giants: a biography of the welfare state* London, Fontana

Conclusion

The research reported in this book conveys a picture of health-related social work at a period of transition. Common themes developed include the need to view health-related social work as much more than hospital related. While hospital activity remains a key focus and symbol of health care, there is no doubt that the community is the location of much health work. Location, however, remains important because it necessitates viewing social work activity in relation to other agencies, professionals and the informal sector of care. All the chapters have referred to this matter of relationships at personal, professional and organisational levels as important, providing evidence that policy on its own will only translate so far in compelling interpersonal, inter-professional and interagency collaboration.

In the short term we predict a range of experiments and localised responses to the future of health-related social work, with a segment of the social work profession valued as hospital social workers in a role which has impressive continuities with their predecessors. We have not included in this text any research from mental health or hospice settings but clearly these areas also value their discrete social work specialities.

In the longer term however we predict a growing merger or marriage (shotgun perhaps) between health and social services activities. These may be part of post-election developments and the successors to the current Government's modernising agendas. At local level these developments will present challenges about the extent to which services are managed or inte-grated and whether mental health work remains under the adult services umbrella. For individual social workers, many of whom have witnessed continual internal organisational restructurings, there will be major changes in relationships, management and work practices.

Such developments can be seen introspectively, and one of social work's contri-butions to these realignments should be its commitment to critical reflection and the necessity for engaging with users' perspectives. There is still little material on what users value in terms of professional skills and attributes. The growth in direct payments for service users looks set to provide us with valuable evidence of what service users want and would prioritise, particularly when resources are limited. We have some evidence from the research reported in this book that service users seek to influence their care despite the difficulties of understand-ing and negotiating complex, changing systems.

The research in this book has pointed to a number of aspects of good practice which are at risk of being neglected in the general flurry of reorganisation and speed of change. It is clear that health-related social workers have a range of skills, experience and knowledge. They often appear to have the trust of service users and to work well with their colleagues, with the rest of social services, within the wider local authority and within other agencies. In some respects their ambiguous position, poised between organisations and locations, may help to confirm their professional independence and ability to advocate on behalf of service users. These are valuable attributes at a time when advocates are in short supply.

The research confirms that social workers in the main take efforts to involve and inform service users and to work with them respecting their choices, valuing independence and meeting needs. Skills such as negotiation, liaison, advocacy and imagination are central to health-related social work. Their knowledge of access points and rights makes them potential allies of service users and also valuable members of a wider professional team.

This book is optimistic about the future of health-related social work, without eulogising the past, and being conscious of the threats to its professional position. The research included here provides evidence of the competence and capacity of social work and challenges those who wish to create new models to include social work values, abilities and capacity. Further work remains to spread aspects of good practice and to learn from service users about what they value.

Index